cholesterol
food, facts and recipes

hamlyn

cholesterol
food, facts and recipes

Juliette Kellow   Recipes by Sara Lewis

CAUTIONS

People with known nut allergies should avoid recipes containing nuts or nut derivatives, and vulnerable people should avoid dishes containing raw or lightly cooked eggs.

Part of the nutritional information provided is salt. These amounts only cover added salt when a specific amount is stated in the recipes.

Heart UK, the cholesterol charity, offers information, support and advice to those who have raised or inherited high cholesterol.

Heart UK
7 North Road
Maidenhead
Berkshire SL6 1PE

Helpline: 0845 450 5988
Website: www.heartuk.org.uk

Nutritional analysis is provided for each recipe and given per serving.

This book is not intended to replace medical care under the direct supervision of a qualified doctor. Before embarking on any changes in your health regime, consult your doctor. While the advice and information are believed to be accurate and true at the time of going to press, neither the author nor the publisher can accept legal responsibility or liability for any errors or omissions that may have been made.

Ovens should be preheated to the specific temperature. If using a fan-assisted oven, follow the manufacturer's instructions for adjusting the time and temperature. Grills should also be preheated.

Both metric and imperial measurements are given for the recipes. Use one set of measurements only, not a mixture of both.

An Hachette Livre UK Company

First published in Great Britain in 2008 by
Hamlyn, a division of Octopus Publishing Group Limited
2–4 Heron Quays, London E14 4JP

Copyright © Octopus Publishing Group Limited 2008

ISBN-13: 978-0-60061-682-5

A CIP catalogue record for this book is available from the British Library

Printed and bound in China

10 9 8 7 6 5 4 3 2 1

contents

introduction

cardiovascular disease and diet

Eating for a healthy heart no longer means filling up on tasteless, boring meals that cut fat out of our diets completely.

The latest dietary advice actively encourages us to eat more of certain foods, such as salmon, avocado, olive oil, wholegrains and an array of fruit and vegetables, to help to lower the risk of heart problems.

It couldn't be better news, given that the latest statistics from the British Heart Foundation reveal that cardiovascular disease – which includes all the diseases of the heart and circulatory system – remains the main cause of death in the UK. Currently, 37 per cent of people in the UK die from the condition every year, most of them

CARDIOVASCULAR DISEASE (CVD)

Stroke

A stroke happens when the blood supply to part of the brain is cut off, depriving it of oxygen and thereby damaging or destroying it and the sufferer.

Peripheral arterial disease (PAD)

A narrowing of the arteries, mainly those carrying blood to the legs, which causes pain when walking. Also known as peripheral vascular disease.

Coronary heart disease (CHD)

Angina

Chest pain or discomfort caused by reduced oxygen supply to the heart, most commonly due to narrowing or partial blocking of the arteries.

Heart attack

When part of the heart muscle dies due to lack of oxygen, usually caused by a blood clot in an artery and occasionally by arterial spasm.

Other diseases:

such as heart murmurs, congenital heart disease and cardiac arrhythmias.

from coronary heart disease (CHD), which includes heart attacks and angina, or strokes. According to the World Health Organization, cardiovascular disease causes 30 per cent of all deaths throughout the world, again predominantly from CHD and stroke.

The four main risk factors for CHD are smoking, high blood cholesterol, high blood pressure and being inactive. Being overweight, having poorly controlled diabetes and drinking too much alcohol also increase the risk. As a rule, the more risk factors we have, the greater our chances of developing CHD. Fortunately, these are all things we can do something about by adapting our lifestyles.

Cholesterol and health

Controlling our blood cholesterol within a healthy range is one of the most important things we can do to reduce our risk of CHD. According to the World Health Organization, raised blood cholesterol is one of the top ten causes of death throughout the world.

This is worrying because the latest figures show that two-thirds – 66 per cent – of adults in the UK have a total cholesterol level above the recommended amount. And, generally, the older we get, the more likely we are to have high total cholesterol. For example, 26 per cent of 16- to 24-year-old males have high total cholesterol, compared with 81 per cent of 45- to 54-year-olds.

It's a misconception, too, that abnormal cholesterol levels are only a problem for men. In the UK, just as many women have high total cholesterol levels as men – in fact, among 16- to 24-year-olds and adults over 55 years, more women have higher cholesterol than men.

The good news is that, if you've picked up this book, you've already taken the first step towards controlling or lowering your blood cholesterol levels, thereby helping to reduce your risk of suffering from a heart attack or angina in later life.

RISK FACTORS FOR CORONARY HEART DISEASE

Things you can do something about:
- Smoking
- High blood cholesterol
- High triglyceride levels
- High blood pressure
- Lack of exercise
- Being overweight or obese
- Drinking too much alcohol
- Poorly controlled diabetes
- Extreme stress

Things you can't change:
- Family history of coronary heart disease
- Getting older
- Being male

what is cholesterol?

You may hear your doctor talking about 'blood lipids'. This is simply a name for all the fatty substances that are found in the blood, including LDL cholesterol, HDL cholesterol and triglycerides.

Cholesterol is found in large amounts in a few foods, such as shellfish, liver and eggs, but most of the cholesterol that circulates in our blood is made in the liver from saturated fats.

Cholesterol is a waxy, fatty material that's an essential part of every cell membrane and is the building block for many important steroid hormones, such as testosterone and progesterone. It's also used to make vitamin D and bile acids, the latter of which help to digest fat. However, if too much cholesterol is made, it can circulate in the blood and increase the risk of CHD.

The cholesterol transport system
Cholesterol uses the blood as its transport system, and travels around the arteries on vehicles made up of proteins. These combinations of cholesterol and proteins are called lipoproteins. There are two main types involved in transporting cholesterol around the body: low density lipoprotein (LDL) and high density lipoprotein (HDL).

LDL or 'bad' cholesterol
LDL transports cholesterol from the liver and drops it off at cells and tissues that need it. However, if there's any damage to the smooth surface of the artery, LDL can also lose some of its cholesterol along the way. The cholesterol that's deposited in the arteries attracts other substances found in the blood, such as dead cells, fibrous tissues, protein and calcium. Together, these form fatty plaques called atheromas. Eventually, these fatty plaques start to clog up our arteries so they become harder and narrower: a process called atherosclerosis.

Consequently, high levels of LDL cholesterol increase the risk of CHD. That's why it's sometimes called 'bad' cholesterol.

HDL or 'good' cholesterol

HDL carries excess cholesterol away from the tissues and arteries to the liver, where the body gets rid of it. High levels of HDL cholesterol protect against heart disease, and for this reason it's sometimes called 'good' cholesterol.

The cholesterol traffic jam

Because cholesterol uses the blood as its transport system, it's our arteries that suffer damage when things go wrong, and ultimately this affects what happens at the final destination, the heart.

When the arteries are narrowed, it's like going from a two-lane dual carriageway to a single-track road. Less blood is able to travel along a narrow road compared to a wider one, so it takes longer to reach its destination.

Blood transports nutrients and oxygen to our organs, including the heart. Anything that restricts its flow means some organs may not receive the oxygen they need to work properly, a condition called ischemia. This is a greater problem when our organs need extra oxygen – during exercise or when we are stressed or very hot. At these times, blood needs to travel more quickly to the organs to supply them with oxygen.

If the coronary arteries – the small vessels that carry blood to the heart – are narrowed, the heart can become deprived of oxygen. This may cause angina characterized by breathlessness and cramp-like pains in the chest, especially during exercise. These pains normally go away when we rest, but are a sign the heart isn't getting enough oxygen.

If fatty plaques in arteries burst, a blood clot can form. If this happens in a narrowed coronary artery, the clot can block the entire artery, effectively causing a traffic jam, and stopping any blood from reaching the heart. When this happens the heart doesn't receive oxygen, resulting in a heart attack.

TRIGLYCERIDES

Triglycerides are another type of fat transported in the blood. They are found in foods like meat, dairy products and cooking oils. After eating, triglycerides from our diet travel around the blood to tissues where they are either used to provide energy or stored as fat. The liver also makes triglycerides if we have too many calories, which the body then stores as fat.

Raised blood triglyceride levels also increase the risk of CHD and stroke, especially when they are combined with high LDL cholesterol and low HDL cholesterol. When triglyceride levels are high, LDL cholesterol becomes more 'dangerous' to the artery linings, speeding up the process of atherosclerosis.

Being overweight, having poorly controlled diabetes, too much fat and/or sugar, drinking too much alcohol and not taking enough exercise can all contribute to high triglyceride levels. The good news is that a healthy diet to reduce cholesterol will also help to reduce triglycerides.

recommended cholesterol levels

Currently in the UK the average total cholesterol level for men is 5.5 mmol/l and for women 5.6 mmol/l, both of which are above the recommended healthy level for total cholesterol.

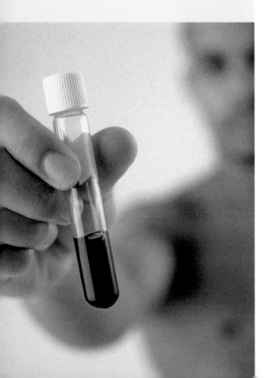

Many of us think high cholesterol levels are bad and low cholesterol levels are good. However, it's a little more complicated than this.

Having high LDL cholesterol is certainly a risk factor for CHD. But having high HDL cholesterol actually helps to protect against it. So, it's more accurate to talk about 'abnormal' rather than 'high' cholesterol levels.

Blood cholesterol and triglyceride levels can be measured at the same time by a simple blood test. Most doctors look at all the blood lipids, which include total cholesterol, LDL and HDL cholesterol and triglycerides, to get a clear picture of potential risk. Because triglyceride levels fluctuate after eating, you will need to avoid all food and drink (except for water) for 12 hours before having a blood test.

In the UK blood lipids are measured in units called millimols per litre of blood, usually shortened to mmol/l. This measures the concentration of cholesterol in each litre of blood. However, in the USA, doctors measure the weight of cholesterol in each 100 ml of blood, so their units are milligrams per decilitre (mg/dL). Healthy levels are as follows:

- ☐ Total cholesterol: less than 5 mmol/l (193 mg/dL)
- ☐ LDL cholesterol: less than 3 mmol/l (116 mg/dL)
- ☐ HDL cholesterol: more than 1 mmol/l (39 mg/dL)
- ☐ Triglycerides: less than 1.7 mmol/l (151 mg/dL)

Your doctor may also work out the ratio of your total cholesterol to your HDL cholesterol by dividing your total cholesterol by your HDL cholesterol. Ideally, this figure should be below 4.5: the higher the figure, the greater the risk of CHD.

Meanwhile, the New Joint British Society Guidelines recommend that for certain people total cholesterol should be limited to 4 mmol/l (154 mg/dL) and LDL to less than 2 mmol/l (77 mg/dL). People who should aim for these lower cholesterol values include anyone with:

- ☐ CHD or a family history of early CHD
- ☐ Other diseases of the heart or circulation
- ☐ High blood pressure or diabetes
- ☐ Abnormal lipid levels

What causes high cholesterol?

About one person in 500 in Britain suffers from an inherited condition that's called familial hypercholesterolemia (FH), which results in exceptionally high cholesterol levels. It's one of the most common genetic disorders in the UK and is caused by an abnormal gene that prevents LDL cholesterol from being removed from the blood as effectively as it should be. This means that adults with FH can have unusually high total blood cholesterol levels, usually 8–12 mmol/l but sometimes much higher. This means they are at risk of suffering with, and dying from, CHD at an early age.

Because it's a genetic condition, FH passes from a parent to a child. There are often few signs or symptoms of the disease, so all close relatives, including children, should get their blood cholesterol levels measured if one person in the family is diagnosed with this condition. A low-fat diet alone is unlikely to lower cholesterol, and most people will also need to take cholesterol-lowering medication.

However, for most people an unhealthy lifestyle and diet are the main causes of high blood cholesterol. Many of the risk factors for CHD (see page 9) are also risk factors for high blood cholesterol. But, in the UK, a poor diet that contains too much saturated fat is considered to be the most common cause of high cholesterol levels. The good news is that this is something we can easily change.

diet and cholesterol

If you have high total cholesterol, it would seem to make sense to eat fewer foods that contain cholesterol. However, this isn't necessarily the case.

A few foods, such as liver, kidney, prawns and eggs, contain more cholesterol than most other foods, so past advice focused on limiting these if you had high blood cholesterol. As eggs tend to be eaten frequently, they were thrown into the spotlight when it came to advising people to cut down on cholesterol-containing foods.

Research now shows that for most, the cholesterol in food has little effect on blood cholesterol. Instead, it's saturated fat that has the biggest impact. Eating fewer foods rich in saturates and making other dietary changes, helps prevent and treat abnormal cholesterol levels. The British Heart Foundation suggests healthy eating can lower cholesterol levels by 5–10 per cent. In most cases the aim is to reduce total cholesterol, by lowering LDL cholesterol, but it's important to raise HDL cholesterol.

Health organizations no longer say that it's necessary to limit the amount of eggs you eat unless your GP has specifically advised you to do so.

eat to beat high cholesterol

- □ Eat less total fat
- □ Swap saturates for polyunsaturates and monounsaturates
- □ Cut back on foods containing trans fats
- □ Eat more fish
- □ Have five fruit and vegetables each day
- □ Eat more foods rich in fibre
- □ Have no more than 6 g (¼ oz) salt a day
- □ Lose weight if you need to
- □ Only drink alcohol in moderation
- □ Take more exercise

eat less total fat

To help reduce cholesterol levels in our bodies, it is important to cut down on the total amount of fat we consume in our everyday diet.

Some fat is necessary for good health and provides fat-soluble vitamins A, D, E and K and essential fats that can't be made in the body. Most people in the UK eat more fat than they need and this can increase blood cholesterol and contribute to excessive weight gain.

In the UK the Department of Health recommends that no more than 33 per cent of our calories should come from fat and no more than a tenth from saturates. This means that if you consume 2,000 calories each day you should have no more than 74 g (3 oz) of fat and 22 g (³/₄ oz) of saturates each day. In the USA healthy eating guidelines recommend that no more than 30 per cent of calories should come from fat and, as in the UK, no more than 10 per cent from saturates.

Recommended daily amounts

In order to help people make healthier food choices in shops and supermarkets, some manufacturers have started labelling their products with guideline daily amounts (GDAs). The GDA is effectively the recommended daily amount that healthy adults need of calories and certain nutrients. Some of these targets – for example, for fat, saturates, sugars and salt – are maximum amounts, so it doesn't matter if you don't actually get this full amount; others – for example, fibre – are amounts we should attempt to meet. The amount of a nutrient contained within a typical serving is then compared to the GDA and expressed as a percentage. The chart on the right shows the GDAs for certain nutrients for men and women.

GUIDELINE DAILY AMOUNTS

	Women	Men
Calories	2,000	2,500
Fat (g)	70	95
Saturates (g)	20	30
Total sugars (g)	90	120
Fibre (g)	18	18
Sodium (g)	2.4	2.4
Salt (g)	6	6

essential facts about fats

easy ways to slash fat

- ☐ Grill, boil, bake, poach, steam, roast without added fat or microwave food instead of frying it.
- ☐ Don't add butter, lard, margarine or oil to food. If you have to use oil, choose olive, rapeseed or sunflower oil and always measure it out.
- ☐ Choose lean cuts of meat and remove all visible fat from meat and the skin from chicken before you eat it.
- ☐ Only use a little butter and margarine. Both contain the same amount of calories and fat – only low-fat spreads contain less.
- ☐ Eat fewer fatty meat products, such as sausages, burgers, pies and pastry products.
- ☐ Cut back on high-fat foods, such as crisps, chocolates, cakes, pastries and biscuits.
- ☐ Use semi-skimmed or skimmed milk only.
- ☐ Opt for low-fat or reduced-fat cheeses.
- ☐ Don't add cream to puddings, sauces or coffee.
- ☐ Choose boiled, mashed or baked potatoes.

Cholesterol-lowering products

It's now possible to buy products such as spreads, milks, yogurts, yogurt drinks and cheeses that claim to reduce cholesterol because they contain naturally occurring plant compounds called sterols or stanols. These added ingredients have a structure similar to cholesterol and there's evidence that they reduce the absorption of cholesterol from the gut, so helping to lower blood cholesterol levels. In particular, they appear to lower both total and LDL cholesterol, but have no effect on HDL cholesterol.

   If you want to give them a go, bear in mind these products are often more expensive than the standard products. They're not a substitute for a healthy diet either. Even if you choose to have spreads, milks, yogurts or drinks that are enriched with plant sterols or stanols, you still need to eat a healthy low-fat diet to reduce your risk of CHD. Sterols and stanols have to be taken in the right quantity to have an effect: 2 g of plant sterols are needed per day, which is roughly the amount you would spread generously on 3 slices of bread (or sparingly on 6).

Labelling low-down

Many products now include additional nutrition information on the packaging to help us make healthier choices. Here's what some of these claims mean:

LABEL	MEANING
Low fat	The food must contain less than 3 g of fat per 100 g
Fat free	The food must contain less than 0.5 g fat per 100 g
Reduced fat	The food must contain 30 per cent less fat than a similar standard product. This doesn't mean the product is low fat, though
Low saturates	The total of the saturated fat and trans fats in the product must be less than 1.5 g saturates per 100 g
Saturates free	The total of the saturated fat and trans fats in the product must be less than 0.1 g saturates per 100 g
Less than 5 per cent fat	The product contains less than 5 g fat per 100 g
Light or lite	The product has to follow the same rules as 'reduced', and the label must outline the characteristics that make it light or lite – for example, a reduction in fat or sugar
Reduced salt or sodium	The product must contain at least 25 per cent less salt or sodium than a similar standard product
Low salt or sodium	The product must contain no more than 0.12 g of sodium or 0.3 g salt per 100 g
Very low salt or sodium	The product must contain no more than 0.04 g sodium or 0.1 g salt per 100 g
Low sugar	The food must contain less than 5 g of sugar per 100 g
No added sugar	No sugars are added, but the product may still contain natural sugars. If the product contains natural sugars, the label must say 'Contains naturally-occurring sugars'
Reduced sugar	The food must contain at least 30 per cent less sugar than a similar standard product

swap saturates for unsaturates

SIMPLE WAYS TO EAT MORE MONOUNSATURATES

- Use olive or rapeseed oil in cooking rather than butter or lard
- In salad dressings, swap mayonnaise or salad cream for olive or rapeseed oil.
- Add avocado to salads or mash it and use in place of butter on sandwiches.
- Make your own guacamole by combining mashed avocado with finely chopped tomato, garlic, lemon juice and Tabasco sauce to taste. Alternatively, you can buy a ready-made version.
- Snack on a handful of unsalted nuts instead of crisps and savoury snacks.
- Add nuts and seeds to salads, stir-fries, curries and pasta dishes.

As well as eating less fat overall, it's important to eat the right types of fat to improve the balance between LDL and HDL cholesterol.

There are three main types of fat in food: saturates, monounsaturates and polyunsaturates. Most foods contain a mixture of these but are generally classified according to the type of fat found in the largest amount.

Saturates

Foods high in saturates include fatty meats, full-fat dairy products, butter, lard, cream, cheese, ghee and coconut and palm oil. Many processed and takeaway foods can also be high in saturates. Saturates are considered to be one of the worst types of fat for increasing the risk of coronary heart disease because they increase LDL or 'bad' cholesterol. As a result, it's important to eat fewer of them.

Polyunsaturates

Polyunsaturated fats can be divided into two groups: omega-3 polyunsaturates and omega-6 polyunsaturates.

Our bodies can make the important long-chain omega-3 fats from foods like rapeseed oil, walnut oil, flaxseeds, nuts, soya and green leafy vegetables. However, oil-rich fish, such as salmon, sardines, mackerel, trout, fresh tuna, pilchards, kippers and herring, are considered to be the best 'ready-made' source of omega-3 fats. These fats lower LDL cholesterol. However, the omega-3 fats in oil-rich fish (see pages 22–23) seem to have even more benefits for heart health, including lowering blood triglycerides.

Omega-6 fats are found in corn, sunflower, soya and fish oils and some margarines and spreads. These fats help to lower LDL cholesterol. Research shows that a balanced intake of both omega-3 and omega-6 fats is important.

tips for keeping red meat healthy

Monounsaturates

Good sources of monounsaturates include olive oil, rapeseed oil, avocados, nuts and seeds. These types of fats lower LDL or 'bad' cholesterol but don't lower levels of HDL or 'good' cholesterol and may actually increase it.

Should I avoid red meat?

In the past some health experts recommended eating less red meat to reduce the risk of high cholesterol because it was considered to be high in fat, particularly saturates. However, over the years, red meat has become much leaner thanks to new breeding programmes and improved butchery techniques. In fact, since the 1950s the fat content of red meat has been significantly reduced, with beef dropping from 25 per cent fat to just 5 per cent fat, pork from 30 per cent fat to 4 per cent fat and lamb from 31 per cent fat to 8 per cent fat.

Most of the red meat we buy today contains more heart-healthy monounsaturates and polyunsaturates than saturates. Meanwhile, choosing lean cuts of meat and trimming off any visible fat helps to reduce the saturated fat content further.

Meat also contains small amounts of omega-3 fats, which help to keep the heart healthy, especially in people who've already had a heart attack. Oily fish, however, is by far the best and healthiest source of omega-3 fats.

+ Choose lean cuts and remove any visible fat before cooking.
+ Opt for a low-fat cooking method and don't add any extra fat.
+ Go for fresh rather than processed meat – it's often lower in fat and usually contains less salt.
+ Stick to small portions – no more than 140 g (4½ oz) a day.
+ Serve meat with plenty of vegetables and starchy, fibre-rich carbs, such as wholewheat pasta, brown rice, wholemeal bread or baked potatoes.

THE AVERAGE FAT CONTENT OF LEAN RED MEAT

Cut of meat	Total fat (g)	Saturates (g)	Monounsaturates (g)	Polyunsaturates (g)
Lean beef	5.1	2.2	2.3	0.3
Lean lamb	8.3	3.8	3.2	0.4
Lean pork	4	1.4	1.5	0.7

Some studies have shown a slight increase in the risk of cardiovascular disease in meat eaters compared with those who don't eat meat. But other studies have shown that eating lean red meat doesn't increase cholesterol, and may even reduce levels of LDL cholesterol. This could possibly be because lean red meat contains monounsaturated fats, omega-3 fats, B vitamins and selenium, all of which help to keep the heart healthy. As a result, in its report on the role that red meat plays in our diets, the British Nutrition Foundation concludes that it's fine to eat lean red meat in moderation and as part of a diet for a healthy heart.

SWAP THIS HIGH SATURATE...	FOR THIS LOW SATURATE ...	SERVING SIZE	SATURATES SAVED
Butter	Sunflower spread	1 teaspoon	1.9 g
Melted lard	Olive oil	1 tablespoon	2.9 g
Full-fat milk	Semi-skimmed milk	200 ml (7 fl oz)	2.8 g
Cheddar cheese	Reduced-fat Cheddar cheese	25 g (1 oz)	3.7 g
Double cream	Low-fat natural yogurt	1 tablespoon	8.8 g
Grilled streaky bacon	Grilled lean back bacon	2 rashers	1.8 g
Minced beef	Extra-lean minced beef	100 g (3$^1/_2$ oz)	2.7 g
Steak and kidney pie	Cottage pie	1 serving	5.6 g
Grilled sausages	Grilled low-fat sausages	2	2.5 g
Cheeseburger	Hamburger	1	2.9 g
Chip-shop chips	Oven chips	165 g (5$^1/_2$ oz)	2.9 g
Cream of tomato soup	Vegetable soup	220 g (7$^1/_2$ oz)	1.1 g
Vanilla ice cream	Lemon sorbet	1 scoop	3.7 g
Danish pastry	Teacake	1	7.8 g

eat fewer trans fats

Information about trans fats has cropped up in the news over the past few years.

These fats occur naturally in small amounts in red meat and dairy products. They are also found in foods that contain hydrogenated fats or hydrogenated vegetable oils.

Typically, foods such as cakes, biscuits, margarines, takeaways, fried foods, pastries and pies contain these added ingredients. Ironically, it's the processing of pure vegetable oils – which are usually a good source of heart-friendly unsaturates – that creates trans fats. During manufacturing, these liquid oils have hydrogen bubbled through them in a process called hydrogenation to improve their texture, flavour and shelf life. The resulting product is a more solid fat, known as hydrogenated fat or hydrogenated vegetable oil, which goes on to be used as an ingredient in many processed foods.

The trans fats that occur naturally in red meat and dairy products don't appear to be harmful to our health. However, research shows that man-made trans fats are as harmful to heart health as saturates, if not more so. Trans fats tend to have a 'triple whammy' effect on blood cholesterol levels: they increase LDL or 'bad' cholesterol, they increase triglycerides, and they lower HDL or 'good' cholesterol. In other words, they're more likely to deposit cholesterol in our arteries while at the same time providing us with fewer resources to mop it up.

As a result, health experts recommend that we should eat fewer foods that contain them. On average, most people in the UK already eat less than the maximum daily amount recommended. However, people who eat a lot of fried and processed foods may be having more than they should. In the meantime, many manufacturers are removing hydrogenated vegetable oils and fats from their products to help us reduce our intake.

HOW CAN I TELL IF FOOD CONTAINS TRANS FATS?

The Department of Health in the UK recommends that no more than 2 per cent of our calories come from trans fats – a value that for most women equates to around 4 g and for men around 6 g a day. However, most food manufacturers in the UK don't label products with grams of trans fats unless they make a specific claim about it on the packaging. This means that you need to scour the ingredients lists for hydrogenated fats or hydrogenated vegetable oils. If a product contains either, it will almost certainly contain trans fats, too – and the higher up the list the ingredient appears, the more trans fats the product will contain. At the same time you should look out for products that label themselves as being 'free from hydrogenated vegetable oil or fat'. These products will usually be free from man-made trans fats.

Man-made trans fats are as harmful to heart health as saturates.

eat more fish

Oil-rich fish like salmon, sardines and mackerel are packed with heart-healthy omega-3 fats.

Health experts advise that everyone should eat two servings of fish every week, at least one of which should be an oil-rich fish.

White fish and shellfish, such as cod, coley, haddock, plaice, sea bass, prawns, crab and scallops, are particularly low in fat, making them a great choice if you want to reduce your total intake of fat. In contrast, as the name suggests, oil-rich fish tend to be higher in fat, particularly omega-3 fats.

The health benefits of oil-rich fish have been the subject of controversy in the past few years, but most experts still believe that they have a crucial role to play in a heart-healthy diet, thanks to their omega-3 fat content. As well as helping to reduce LDL cholesterol, omega-3 fats have been shown to have many other benefits for the heart, including:

- Reducing the stickiness of blood, so that it's less likely to clot.
- Helping to keep the heart beating regularly.
- Protecting the small arteries that carry blood to the heart from damage.
- Lowering levels of triglycerides.
- Improving the chances of survival after a heart attack.

In fact, the heart health benefits of oil-rich fish are considered to be so important that people who suffer with angina or have had a heart attack should have two to three portions each week.

tasty ways to eat more oil-rich fish

- ☐ Fill a wholegrain bagel with smoked salmon and a little reduced-fat soft cheese.
- ☐ Top toast with a small can of sardines or mackerel in tomato sauce for lunch.
- ☐ Try a fresh tuna steak for dinner: grill it and serve it with a baked potato, salad and a squeeze of lemon.
- ☐ Mix canned pink salmon with cooked wholewheat pasta, lightly steamed broccoli and reduced-fat soft cheese with garlic and herbs, heat through and serve with salad.
- ☐ Make your own smoked mackerel pâté by mixing smoked mackerel with lemon juice, fat-free fromage frais and fresh tarragon, and then serve it with wholemeal toast and salad for lunch.
- ☐ Look out for salmon fishcakes in your local supermarket. Cook them according to the instructions on the pack and serve with salad.
- ☐ Make your own fish fingers or goujons with fresh salmon.
- ☐ Look for pre-prepared, ready-to-cook packs of trout, mackerel or salmon in the supermarket. The packaging will provide cooking instructions.
- ☐ Enjoy a posh brunch at the weekend by adding smoked salmon to scrambled eggs. Serve on wholegrain muffins or bagels.

what counts as oily fish?

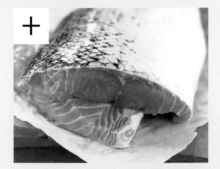

- + Salmon
- + Trout
- + Mackerel
- + Herring
- + Sardines
- + Pilchards
- + Kipper
- + Fresh tuna*
- + Anchovies
- + Swordfish

*Fresh tuna is rich in omega-3 fats, but when it's canned these fats are reduced to levels similar to white fish. This means that only fresh tuna can be regarded as an oil-rich fish. However, canned tuna still counts as one of the two weekly portions of fish recommended.

eat five fruit and vegetables a day

All fruit and vegetables, including fresh, frozen, canned, dried, pure juices and smoothies count towards the five recommended daily servings.

Health experts recommend that we eat five servings of fruit and vegetables a day.

Most fruit and vegetables are low in fat and high in fibre (see pages 29–31), both of which are important for a healthy heart and helping with weight loss, if necessary. But many fruit and vegetables are also packed with antioxidants, which research shows may help to protect against CHD.

Antioxidants such as beta-carotene, vitamins C and E, and selenium, 'mop up' an excess of potentially harmful molecules called free radicals. Free radicals are created naturally in the day-to-day workings of our bodies. However, our lifestyles can influence the amount of free radicals that are made. Smoking and pollution, for example, can both cause an excess of free radicals. This is particularly bad news for our hearts as it's thought that free radicals cause oxidation of LDL cholesterol, allowing it to settle more easily in the artery walls, which in turn speeds up the process of the narrowing of arteries. Antioxidant nutrients are, therefore, particularly important because they help to rid the body of an excess of free radicals.

In addition, many fruits and vegetables are good sources of phytochemicals, naturally occurring plant chemicals that are also powerful antioxidants. In particular, a group of phytochemicals called flavonoids have been studied extensively. Flavonoids are found in many different fruits and vegetables, especially apples and onions. As well as helping to reduce the oxidation of LDL cholesterol, research also suggests that flavonoids may help to make blood less sticky, therefore potentially reducing the chances of getting a blood clot.

Meanwhile, another phytochemical, lycopene, has also received a lot of attention for its potential role in keeping the heart healthy thanks to it being a potent antioxidant. Lycopene is found in tomatoes, red grapefruit,

hidden benefits inside fruit and vegetables

guava and watermelon, but, as the body is better able to absorb lycopene when it's in cooked foods, processed products, such as canned tomatoes, tomato purée and tomato-based sauces, tend to be better sources of this antioxidant than the fresh ingredients.

Some vitamins and minerals found in fruit and vegetables may also have a role in helping to keep our hearts healthy. For example, most fruit and vegetables are rich in potassium, a mineral that helps to control blood pressure and keeps the heart beating regularly. Green vegetables – spinach, sprouts, watercress, asparagus, kale and broccoli, for instance – and citrus fruit are also a good source of a B vitamin called folic acid, which reduces levels of a substance called homocysteine in the blood. This is important because raised levels of homocysteine, which is caused by the breakdown of an amino acid called methionine, increase the risk of CHD. Too much homocysteine in the blood has a double effect on heart health: first, it's converted into a compound that combines with LDL cholesterol to form fatty plaques; and second, it sets off changes in the lining of the artery that may cause blood clots.

What counts as a portion?

All fruit and vegetables, including fresh, frozen, canned, dried and pure juices, count towards the five recommended daily servings. The only exception is potatoes, which are a starchy food and so are not included in the recommended five a day. Meanwhile, no matter how much you drink, a glass of juice counts as one portion. This is because, unlike fresh, frozen, canned or dried fruit and vegetables, juices don't contain much fibre. In addition, juicing 'squeezes out' the natural sugars normally found between the cells of fruit or vegetables, making juices less healthy for your teeth. Pulses, such as kidney beans, lentils and

Garlic is a great way to flavour food without the need to add salt – and cutting down on salt can help to lower blood pressure, which is a risk factor for CHD.

chickpeas, also only count as one portion, no matter how many you eat. This is because they don't contain the same vitamins and minerals as other fruit and vegetables. They are rich in soluble fibre, however, which can help reduce cholesterol absorption (see page 29)

It's important to eat five different fruit and vegetables each day to get a wide range of vitamins and minerals. As a guide, the more colours you go for, the greater the variety of nutrients you'll get. For example, you could have a glass of orange juice for breakfast, add a tomato to a sandwich at lunchtime, serve dinner with two vegetables, such as carrots and broccoli, and snack on an apple. It's as easy as that!

A portion of fruit or vegetable is equivalent to around 75 g (3 oz). The fruit and vegetables included in cooked dishes all count. Below are some examples of what counts as one portion:
- ☐ 1 apple, banana, pear or orange
- ☐ 2 plums, satsumas or kiwifruits
- ☐ ½ grapefruit or avocado
- ☐ 1 large slice of melon or fresh pineapple
- ☐ 3 heaped tablespoons of vegetables, beans or pulses
- ☐ 3 heaped tablespoons of fruit salad or stewed fruit
- ☐ 1 heaped tablespoon of raisins or sultanas
- ☐ 3 dried apricots
- ☐ 1 cupful of grapes, cherries or berries
- ☐ 1 dessert bowl of salad
- ☐ 150 ml (¼ pint) pure fruit or vegetable juice

Is garlic good for a healthy heart?
According to the British Heart Foundation, there's currently not enough evidence to suggest that garlic can protect us from heart disease. Nevertheless, together with fresh herbs, garlic is a great way to flavour food without the need to add salt – and cutting down on salt can help to lower blood pressure, which is a risk factor for CHD.

easy ways to eat more fruit and vegetables

☐ Keep your fruit bowl full and easily accessible.
☐ Add extra vegetables to dishes such as curries, casseroles, cottage pie, pasta dishes, chilli, ready-meals, pizzas, sauces and soups.
☐ Instead of creating a salad from scratch, buy bags of ready-prepared salad leaves.
☐ Keep bags of frozen vegetables and berries in the freezer for days when you run out of fresh – they contain just as many nutrients as fresh.
☐ Think about ordering a box of fruit and vegetables each week.
☐ Find new ways to cook vegetables, especially those you think you don't like.
☐ Try some of the more exotic fruit and vegetables, such as mango, pomegranate, dragon fruit, pak choi, butternut squash, fennel and celeriac.
☐ Keep salads interesting by using different types of leaf and adding ingredients, such as peppers, onions, sweetcorn, avocado, radishes, peas, grated carrot and cabbage.
☐ Snack on carrot sticks, sliced pepper, cherry tomatoes, mushrooms or cauliflower florets, with reduced-fat hummus or tzatziki.
☐ Serve up puddings such as wholemeal fruit crumbles, canned fruit in sugar-free jelly, baked apples or sliced banana with low-fat custard.
☐ Turn some of your favourite dishes vegetarian: try vegetarian lasagne, mushroom risotto and potato and cauliflower curry.
☐ Make fresh fruit smoothies with your favourite types of fruit.

Should I eat more soya?

Soya products might not make it into many of our shopping trolleys, but there's some evidence they may keep our heart healthy. Studies show that including 25 g (1 oz) of soya protein each day as part of a diet low in saturates can help to slightly lower both total cholesterol and LDL cholesterol. Meanwhile, soya products also tend to be a good source of soluble fibre (see page 29) and flavonoids, both of which have been linked with a healthy heart. However, it's worth bearing in mind that eating more soya alone is unlikely to have a major impact on lowering cholesterol. You will still need to eat a healthy, low-fat diet, lose weight if necessary and take more exercise.

You can get 25 g (1 oz) of soya protein by drinking around three glasses (about 1¼ pints) of soya milk a day, but make sure you choose unsweetened, calcium-fortified varieties. There are also many soya desserts, yogurt alternatives and creams available, but always check the nutrition information because they may be higher in calories than you'd expect. It's also a good idea to include soya products in addition to regular dairy products so that you continue to get all the beneficial nutrients supplied by milk.

WHERE TO FIND ANTIOXIDANT NUTRIENTS

Nutrient	Where to find it
Selenium	Meat, fish, poultry, nuts and seeds
Beta-carotene	Dark green vegetables, like spinach and watercress, and yellow, orange and red vegetables and fruit, like carrots, tomatoes, dried apricots, sweet potatoes and mangoes
Vitamin C	Blackcurrants, berries, green leafy vegetables, like Brussels sprouts, cabbage, spinach and broccoli, tomatoes, peppers, kiwifruit, citrus fruit and their juices
Vitamin E	Vegetable oils, spreads, avocados, nuts, seeds, green leafy vegetables, eggs and wholegrains

eat more fibre-rich foods

Eating more fibre-rich foods doesn't just keep our digestive system in good working order. It's also important for a healthy heart.

Most foods that contain good amounts of fibre are low in fat and contain a range of heart-friendly vitamins, minerals and phytochemicals. Moreover, a diet that contains good amounts of fibre can help us to control our weight or lose it by keeping us fuller for longer so we're less likely to snack. This is particularly important because weight loss can help to reduce blood cholesterol. Dietary fibre can be divided into two main types: insoluble and soluble.

Insoluble fibre
This type of fibre helps to keep the digestive system healthy by increasing the bulk and softness of the stools, which, in turn, assists the smooth passage of food through the body. It's this type of fibre that helps to prevent complaints like constipation, piles, diverticular disease and possibly even bowel cancer.

Insoluble fibre also helps to fill us up. It acts like a sponge and absorbs and holds on to water. This means fibre-rich foods swell in our stomach to make us feel fuller and prevent hunger. Foods rich in insoluble fibre include wholemeal flour and bread, wholegrain breakfast cereals, bran, brown rice, wholemeal pasta, grains, nuts, seeds and some fruit and vegetables.

Soluble fibre
Soluble fibre also has a role to play in helping to control our weight. It forms a gel in the intestine, which is thought to slow down the digestion and absorption of carbohydrates, such as glucose. This means that it helps to keep blood sugar levels steady, preventing carb

Soluble fibre may have a specific role to play in keeping our hearts healthy by helping to lower blood cholesterol.

EASY WAYS TO EAT MORE FIBRE

- Start your day with a bowl of porridge or high-fibre cereal.
- Have at least five servings of fruit and vegetables each day and eat the skins on fruits like apples and pears and scrub vegetables like carrots and parsnips rather than peeling them.
- Don't peel potatoes. Serve jacket potatoes, wedges or boiled new potatoes in their skins rather than chips or mash.
- Add barley or lentils to stews, soups and casseroles.
- Add peas or beans to stir-fries and salads or enjoy beans on toast for breakfast or lunch.
- Swap white pasta, rice, noodles and bread for the brown varieties.
- If you like baking, try replacing some or all of the white flour in the recipe for wholemeal flour.
- Top fruit salad and yogurt with oats, muesli or crunchy granola.
- Swap crisps, chocolate and biscuits for high-fibre snacks such as unsalted nuts and seeds, dried or fresh fruit or low-fat dips with vegetable crudités.
- Start your evening meal with a high-fibre starter, such as mixed salad, corn-on-the-cob, vegetable or bean soup, vegetable kebabs, melon, avocado with crab or roasted vegetables.

cravings that leave many of us reaching for sugary snacks that are also often combined with fat, such as biscuits, chocolate, buttered toast and jam, muffins and doughnuts. In addition, it can help to control blood sugar levels in people with diabetes.

But that's not all. Soluble fibre is also thought to have a specific role in keeping our hearts healthy by helping to lower blood cholesterol. It's thought that this type of fibre binds with cholesterol to prevent it from being reabsorbed into the bloodstream. This lowers the amount of cholesterol in the blood, thereby reducing the risk of CHD.

An analysis of ten trials has shown that 3 g of soluble fibre each day from oats (one of the main sources of soluble fibre) can help to lower blood cholesterol slightly. Other foods that are rich in soluble fibre include fruit, vegetables, barley and pulses, such as beans, lentils and peas.

How much fibre?

When it comes to staying healthy, it's best to eat a range of fibre-rich foods, rather than just one or two sources. This means you'll get a mixture of both soluble and insoluble fibre and so enjoy the health benefits offered by both. As a guide, look at food labels to help you identify those foods that contain good amounts of fibre. The Department of Health recommends that adults eat an average of 18 g of fibre a day with a range of 12–24 g.

Go with the grain

Experts now recommend eating more wholegrains. Several large studies in the USA, Finland and Norway have found that people who eat relatively large amounts of wholegrain cereals have significantly lower rates of heart attacks and stroke.

As the name suggests, wholegrain foods contain all the grain, including the nutrient-rich germ, the energy-providing endosperm and the fibre-rich bran layer. When grains are refined – to make white flour, rice or bread, for example – the outer bran layer and germ of the grain are stripped away with the result that the grain loses much of its fibre and many of its nutrients. In fact, it's becoming increasingly clear that it's the combination of fibre, vitamins, minerals, phytochemicals, antioxidants and complex carbohydrates that gives wholegrain foods their many health benefits.

Wholegrains and a healthy heart

The benefits of wholegrains to heart health are now considered to be so well established that foods containing at least 51 per cent wholegrain by weight can carry the following claim on their label: 'People with a healthy heart tend to eat more wholegrain foods as part of a healthy lifestyle.'

Wholegrains benefit our health in other ways, too. Research shows that they help to maintain healthy blood sugar levels and keep the digestive system healthy. People who eat more wholegrain foods are more likely to have a lower Body Mass Index (BMI) and are less likely to gain weight over time.

Thanks to all of these benefits, many health experts now recommend eating three servings of wholegrains a day. One serving contains 16 g of wholegrain and is equivalent to:

- ☐ 1 medium slice of wholemeal bread
- ☐ 1 small wholemeal roll
- ☐ 1 small bowl of porridge
- ☐ 1 Shredded Wheat or Weetabix
- ☐ 3 tablespoons wholegrain cereal
- ☐ 3 heaped tablespoons wholewheat pasta
- ☐ 2 heaped tablespoons boiled brown rice
- ☐ ½ wholemeal pitta bread
- ☐ 2–3 cups plain popcorn
- ☐ 3–4 small wholegrain rice cakes or rye crispbreads

People with a healthy heart tend to eat more wholegrain foods as part of a healthy lifestyle.

cut down on salt

High blood pressure is a risk factor for heart disease so it's important to keep it under control. Research shows that people with high blood pressure are three times more likely to develop heart disease or have a stroke than people with normal blood pressure.

High salt intakes themselves don't increase cholesterol levels, but they do increase blood pressure, which, like smoking, inactivity and high blood cholesterol, is a risk factor for CHD.

High blood pressure means the heart has to work harder to pump blood around the body, and as a result it can become overworked and damaged, potentially increasing the risk of a heart attack. High blood pressure is also common in people with atherosclerosis because the blood has to be pumped through narrow, less flexible arteries, which in turn increases the pressure in these blood vessels (see page 10).

There's now overwhelming scientific evidence that eating less salt can help to lower blood pressure. Most of us eat around 9 g of salt every day, but for a healthy heart we should limit this to just 6 g a day. In particular, it's the sodium component of salt (also known as sodium chloride) that's linked to high blood pressure.

The problem is that most of this sodium no longer comes from the salt cellar. In fact, just 10 per cent of salt is added in cooking or at the table, with a further 15 per cent coming from natural sources. Processed foods account for three-quarters of the salt in our diet. Consequently, the key to lowering sodium intakes is to eat fewer salty, processed foods, such as sauces, pickles, ready-meals, ready-made pasta sauces, canned soups, burgers, sausages, bacon, smoked foods, chicken nuggets, pizzas, takeaways, crisps and savoury snacks. Moreover, foods like bread, breakfast cereals and cheese can also be packed with salt even though they usually contain good amounts of vitamins and minerals, too. This means that it's important to opt for products that contain the least salt.

easy ways to slash salt

- ☐ Ban the salt cellar from your kitchen and table.
- ☐ Eat fewer salty and processed foods, such as sauces, crisps, burgers, sausages, pizzas, takeaways, canned soups and ready-meals.
- ☐ Make your own low-salt 'ready-meals'. Freeze leftover homemade lasagne, chilli, Bolognese sauce, soups, casseroles and cauliflower cheese, so that you have a constant supply of low-salt meals for evenings when you don't have time to cook.
- ☐ Make your own burgers using extra-lean minced beef and fresh herbs and spices.
- ☐ Buy vegetables canned in water rather than those with added salt, or stick with frozen vegetables. Steam rather than boil fresh vegetables, as you'll be less likely to add salt.
- ☐ Don't use salt in cooking. Instead, flavour food with herbs, garlic, spices, ginger, lime, lemon juice and black pepper. Use different onions, such as red onions, spring onions and shallots to flavour dishes.
- ☐ Marinate meat, fish and poultry in salt-free marinades to add flavour.
- ☐ Make your own fresh stocks and gravy instead of using stock cubes or gravy granules. Alternatively, look for lower salt products.
- ☐ Add a little red or white wine to stews, casseroles, risottos and pasta sauces.
- ☐ Compare the salt content of similar products in the supermarket and opt for lower salt products. Many manufacturers have started to reduce the salt content of some of their products and have started producing lower salt alternatives.

HOW MUCH SALT IS IN FOODS?

Unfortunately, not all foods are labelled with values for salt, so you need to do the sums. Multiply the value for sodium in a portion by 2.5 to give you the total amount of salt in that portion. As a simple guide, the Food Standards Agency suggest that foods with 1.25 g of salt or 0.5 g of sodium per 100 g or more are high in salt, while those containing 0.25 g salt or 0.1 g sodium per 100 g or less are low in salt.

COOKING WITH LOW-SALT STOCK

When recipes require stock and you use cubes or powder, always check the labelling to find low-salt and reduced-stock brands. Vegetable cubes contain less salt than chicken cubes or bouillon powder. If you have time, make your own stock and add no salt at all.

drink alcohol in moderation

Binge drinking may also cause abnormal heart rhythms, and regular heavy drinking can enlarge the heart.

Despite the widely held belief that red wine is good for the heart, most experts agree that eating a healthy diet, stopping smoking and being more active are likely to have a far greater benefit to the health of our hearts than drinking alcohol.

According to the British Heart Foundation, one or two units of alcohol a day may help to protect against heart disease – but only in men over the age of 40 and postmenopausal women. Alcohol helps to raise HDL or 'good' cholesterol, although this can also be achieved by taking more exercise, and alcohol may reduce the stickiness of the blood, helping to reduce the risk of blood clots.

However, people who persistently exceed sensible drinking limits – that's a maximum of three units a day for women and four units a day for men – are more likely to suffer from conditions such as high blood pressure, which increase the risk of having a heart attack or stroke. Alcohol also contains calories, but little else in the way of nutrients, so drinking large amounts can contribute to being overweight or obese, also a risk factor for coronary heart disease. Binge drinking may also cause abnormal heart rhythms, and regular heavy drinking can enlarge the heart.

While some research has suggested that red wine is the most beneficial alcohol for heart health, because it contains flavonoids (see page 24), this is still not conclusive. Indeed, it is now thought that small amounts of any alcohol are associated with a lower risk of heart disease, and it may be that drinking alcohol with meals is more beneficial to health than drinking it on its own.

top tips for drinking sensibly

☐ Start off with a couple of soft drinks. It's not unusual to be thirsty when you first arrive at a bar, club or restaurant, so quench this thirst with alcohol-free beverages.

☐ Mix wine with soda or sparkling water and ice to make it last longer.

☐ Don't drink neat spirits – always add a mixer, such as diet cola, slimline tonic or orange juice.

☐ Have one soft drink after every alcoholic one.

☐ Don't be afraid to skip rounds, and when it's your turn, buy a non-alcoholic drink for yourself. If friends pressure you to keep drinking, tell them it's an alcoholic drink – a lemonade looks just like a gin and tonic!

☐ Avoid doubles and watch out for bars that serve them as standard. Many pubs now also sell 35 ml (1½ fl oz) measures as the standard instead of the more usual 25 ml (1 fl oz) measure. These contain around 1.5 units.

☐ Use a spirits measure for drinks at home rather than pouring freely from the bottle.

☐ Avoid strong beer, lager and cider and opt for the standard strength ones instead.

☐ Give cocktails a miss. Although packed with alcohol, the mixers often mean that they don't taste alcoholic so it's easy to overindulge.

☐ You can calculate the units of alcohol in a bottle or can of drink by multiplying the %ABV given on the bottle by the amount of the drink in millilitres. Then divide by 1,000.

☐ Remember that most alcoholic drinks are high in calories so won't do your weight any favours!

DRINK SENSIBLY

For good health the Department of Health in the UK recommends that men should not drink more than 3–4 units of alcohol a day and that women should have no more than 2–3 units a day. That might sound a lot, but it's easy to have your entire daily unit intake in just one drink. The list below shows the number of units of alcohol contained in some common drinks:

- 600 ml (1 pint) ordinary strength beer, lager or cider = 2 units
- 600 ml (1 pint) strong beer, lager or cider = 3 units
- 175 ml (6 fl oz) red or white wine = 2 units
- 25 ml (1 fl oz) pub measure of spirits = 1 unit
- 1 bottle of alcopop = approximately 1.5 units

maintain a healthy weight

Being overweight or obese is a risk factor for coronary heart disease in itself, but weighing too much also increases the chances of developing high blood cholesterol, high blood pressure and diabetes, all of which increase the risk of heart disease.

One of the easiest ways to identify whether you are a healthy weight for your height is to know your Body Mass Index (BMI). Your GP or practice nurse will be able to work this out for you, or visit the British Dietetic Association's Weight Wise website at www.bdaweightwise.com and enter your weight and height into its BMI calculator. Alternatively, it's easy to work it out yourself if you have a calculator and know your weight in kilograms and your height in metres (see below left).

As well as calculating your BMI, measure your waist circumference to check where the fat is distributed on your body. Being an 'apple' shape, where fat is stored around your middle, increases the risk of health problems like coronary heart disease, high blood pressure and diabetes. To measure your waist circumference, use a tape measure to measure along the line of your belly button. A waist circumference of 80 cm (32 in) for women and 94 cm (37 in) for men means you are at an increased risk of health problems. A waist measurement of 88 cm (35 in) for women and 102 cm (40 in) for men means you are at a high risk and should consider losing weight.

The good news is that even small weight losses of 5–10 per cent of bodyweight will benefit your health. This means, for example, that someone who weighs 83 kg (13 stone) will benefit from losing just 4–8 kg (9–18 lb) if they are overweight to start with.

WORKING OUT YOUR BMI

To calculate your Body Mass Index multiply your height (in metres) squared, then divide your weight in kilograms by the figure you've just calculated. For example, if you weigh 83 kg (13 st) and are 1.7 m high (5 ft 7 in), the calculation is $83 \div (1.7 \times 1.7) = 28.7$.

- A BMI of 18.5 indicates you are underweight.
- A BMI of 18.5 to 24.9 is healthy.
- A BMI of 25 to 29.9 indicates you are overweight.
- A BMI of over 30 indicates you are obese.

The higher your BMI, the greater the risk to your health.

How do I lose weight?

Eating a balanced diet that is low in fat and high in fibre is a good starting point, but to shift that excess weight you also need to create a calorie deficit or shortfall – in other words, you need to take in fewer calories than you use up so that your body draws on its fat stores to provide it with the energy it needs to function properly.

The easiest way to create this calorie deficit is to reduce your daily calorie intake *and* burn more calories by increasing daily activity levels. To lose 500 g (1 lb) of fat each week you need to create a calorie deficit of just 500 calories a day. That might sound like a lot, but it can be easily achieved by simply swapping butter on two slices of toast for low-fat spread, having an apple instead of a large packet of crisps, replacing a tablespoon of mayonnaise on salad for fat-free dressing and walking briskly for 20 minutes.

You should aim to lose no more than 500 g–1 kg (1–2 lb) a week. It's easier and healthier to lose weight slowly, and you'll be far more likely to keep the weight off in the long run.

One of the simplest ways to reduce calories is to eat fewer fatty foods. Compared to carbohydrates and protein, fat contains more than twice as many calories per gram – around 9 kcal compared with 4 kcal. As a result, foods that are high in fat are also usually high in calories. All fat contains the same amount of calories, too. For example, despite containing fewer saturates and more monounsaturates, a tablespoon of olive oil has a similar calorie content to a tablespoon of melted lard. So if you want to lose weight, it's important to cut down on all types of fat – not just those that are high in saturates.

However, don't be fooled into thinking that all foods described as 'low-fat' or 'fat-free' (see page 17) are automatically low in calories or calorie-free. Some low-fat products can be higher in calories than standard

Not all 'low-fat' or 'fat-free' products are automatically low in calories, so always check food labels.

products because they contain extra sugars and thickeners to add flavour and texture. The solution: always check the calorie content of low-fat foods, especially things like cakes, biscuits, crisps, ice creams and ready-meals. You might find there's little difference in the calorie content when you compare it to the standard product.

Meanwhile, it's also important to cut calories from foods that contain few other nutrients. Fizzy drinks, sugar, biscuits, cake, chocolate and crisps simply add 'empty' calories to your diet without much protein, fibre, vitamins or minerals. Instead, focus on getting calories from nutrient-rich foods, such as lean meat, fish, lower fat dairy products and high-fibre carbs.

SIMPLE CALORIE SWAPS

Swap ...	For ...	Serving size	Save ...
Full-fat milk (130 calories)	Semi-skimmed milk (92 calories)	200 ml (7 fl oz)	38 calories
Sunflower margarine (35 calories)	Low-fat spread (20 calories)	1 teaspoon	15 calories
Cheddar cheese (124 calories)	Reduced-fat Cheddar cheese (78 calories)	30 g (1¼ oz)	46 calories
Olive oil (100 calories)	Spray oil (10 calories)	Equivalent of 1 tablespoon	90 calories
Sugar (16 calories)	Artificial sweetener (0 calories)	Equivalent of 1 teaspoon	16 calories
Mayonnaise (105 calories)	Fat-free dressing (10 calories)	1 tablespoon	95 calories
Regular sandwich (600 calories)	Low-fat sandwich (350 calories)	1 pack	250 calories
Cola (135 calories)	Diet cola (0 calories)	1 can	135 calories
Chocolate digestive biscuits (270 calories)	3 plums (60 calories)	3	210 calories
Total calorie saving			895 calories

manage stress

While a healthy diet is often considered to be the main ingredient for a healthy heart, most experts believe that it's only one part of the recipe.

Even as far back as the 1950s, Professor Ancel Keys recognized that lifestyle factors as well as diet probably play a role in keeping the heart healthy. And that includes a slower pace of life and less stress.

When we are stressed, our bodies release the hormone adrenaline into the blood, and this extra adrenaline increases our blood pressure, heart rate and blood flow and allows more air into the lungs. This is obviously important in situations where we may need to remove ourselves from danger. However, most of the stressful situations that cause this reaction in modern life – work overload, exams, interviews, relationship problems, moving house or getting married – don't need us to flee from danger. Nevertheless, many of us are constantly on 'red alert', and unfortunately this stress reaction puts the heart under tremendous pressure as it works harder to pump blood around the body more quickly. Being stressed alone won't cause a heart attack, but problems may be more likely if there is an underlying heart problem such as atherosclerosis.

Equally important, stress can affect our diet, exercise, drinking and smoking habits. For example, in times of stress, many of us may smoke or drink more, take less exercise or eat a poor diet that's packed with fatty and sugary foods and few fruit and vegetables. In turn, all of these can increase our risk factors for CHD, such as increasing blood cholesterol and blood pressure or contributing to unwanted weight gain. The solution is to find ways to combat stress.

TOP TIPS TO BEAT STRESS

- Take regular exercise. Aim for at least 30 minutes five times a week.
- Don't bottle things up. Talk to family, friends or colleagues if there are problems or issues.
- Consider taking part in relaxation classes, such as yoga or meditation.
- Indulge in some relaxing 'me time', such as soaking in the bath or reading your favourite magazine.
- Avoid smoking or drinking more alcohol. The chances are that you'll worry about this, adding to your stress.
- Eat regularly and don't skip meals. Low blood sugar levels will make you feel tired, irritable, hungry, and even less able to cope with stressful situations.
- Include plenty of fibre-rich, starchy carbs to keep your blood sugar levels steady between meals.
- Drink plenty of water. Dehydration makes it harder to concentrate and focus on tasks, so they take even longer to complete.
- Learn to manage your time more effectively and don't be afraid to say 'no'.
- If your stress levels are extremely high, consider some stress counselling or stress management sessions.

get active

It's important to consult your doctor before starting a new exercise plan, especially if you haven't exercised for a long time, have had a heart attack or angina or think you may be at risk of coronary heart disease.

Being more active can help to lower or control many of the risk factors for coronary heart disease.

Research reveals that people who are inactive are twice as likely to have a heart attack as those who exercise regularly. Exercise can help to lower blood pressure, reduce resting heart rate and combat stress (see page 39). It can also help with weight control or weight loss if necessary, and it can reduce the risk of developing type 2 diabetes or help to control the condition. In addition, regular exercise helps to increase levels of HDL or 'good' cholesterol and lowers levels of LDL or 'bad' cholesterol within the body.

To gain the most benefits, it's important to do 30 minutes of moderate-intensity activity at least five times a week. This could include brisk walking, jogging, dancing, swimming or cycling. You don't need to exercise to the point of exhaustion either – exercise should leave you warm and a bit out of breath, but you should still be able to talk.

If you haven't exercised before, it's crucial to start slowly and gradually increase the amount and intensity of your activities. It's also important to build more activity into your daily routines. Health experts recommend that we should take 10,000 steps every day. It might not sound much, but it's equivalent to about 8 kilometres (5 miles). Unfortunately, most of us are not even close to achieving this, with many of us doing as little as 3,000 steps a day. Investing in a pedometer will help you work out how many daily steps you are taking. Simply clip it to the waistband of your trousers or skirt in the morning and let it count the number of steps you walk each day. Once you have an idea of your daily step count you can gradually work towards increasing this, until you reach the daily target of 10,000 steps.

easy ways to get more active

☐ Forget the car or bus and walk to the shop, school or post office.

☐ Park on the opposite side of the supermarket car park so you have to walk further to and from the entrance.

☐ Never use lifts or escalators – take the stairs instead.

☐ Plug the phone in upstairs so that you have to climb a flight of steps to answer it or make a call.

☐ Pull on your trainers at lunchtime and go for a brisk 30-minute walk.

☐ Stop using online shopping and banking services and instead go to the supermarket, shopping centre or bank in person to do all your chores.

☐ In the office deliver internal messages in person rather than using e-mail or the phone and go to the post room yourself when there's a delivery rather than getting someone else to do it.

☐ Make your social life more active. For example, swap nights out in the pub or at a restaurant for a sauna and swim, dancing lessons or ten-pin bowling.

☐ Turn exercise into a fun family event. Go for a family swim or cycle, have a game of football or Frisbee in the park, or pack up a picnic and go for a walk in the country.

☐ Turn off the TV and do something more active – digging out the dance mat or playing Twister will get your heart working harder than simply staring at a screen.

It's important to do 30 minutes of moderate-intensity activity at least five times a week. This could include brisk walking, jogging, dancing, swimming or cycling.

light
lunches

Nutritional values

Kcals 231

fat 7.7 g

saturates 1.6 g

sugars 6.1 g

salt 0.6 g

Preparation time

30 minutes

Cooking time

56 minutes

Serves

4

✚ **NUTRITIONAL TIP**

Rather than buying a can of spray oil, make your own by recycling a well-washed, pump-action spray bottle and fill it with olive oil or buy a new, small, plastic make-up atomizer. Ideal for roast potatoes, too.

Tomato, red lentil & cumin soup

This chunky, spiced soup is flavoured with cumin and chilli powder. If you can find it, use the delicious Spanish smoked paprika (pimenton), which is now widely available in supermarkets, instead of the chilli powder.

1 tablespoon sunflower oil

1 onion, finely chopped

2 garlic cloves, finely chopped

1½ teaspoons cumin seeds, roughly crushed

1 teaspoon chilli powder or smoked pimenton

375 g (12 oz) tomatoes, chopped

100 g (3½ oz) red lentils

1.2 litres (2 pints) low-salt vegetable stock

pepper

Croutons
75 g (3 oz) sesame wholemeal torpedo roll, cubed

1 tablespoon sunflower oil

little chilli powder or smoked pimenton

1 Heat the oil in a saucepan, add the onion and fry for 5 minutes or until softened and just beginning to brown. Stir in the garlic, cumin and chilli or pimenton and cook for 1 minute.

2 Mix in the tomatoes, lentils, stock and a little pepper and bring to the boil. Stir well, then cover and simmer for 45 minutes or until the lentils are tender.

3 Meanwhile, make the croutons. Put the bread on a baking sheet, spray with the oil, then sprinkle with chilli or pimenton. Bake in a preheated oven, 200°C (400°F), Gas Mark 6, for 5 minutes or until crisp and golden.

4 Ladle the soup into bowls and top with the croutons.

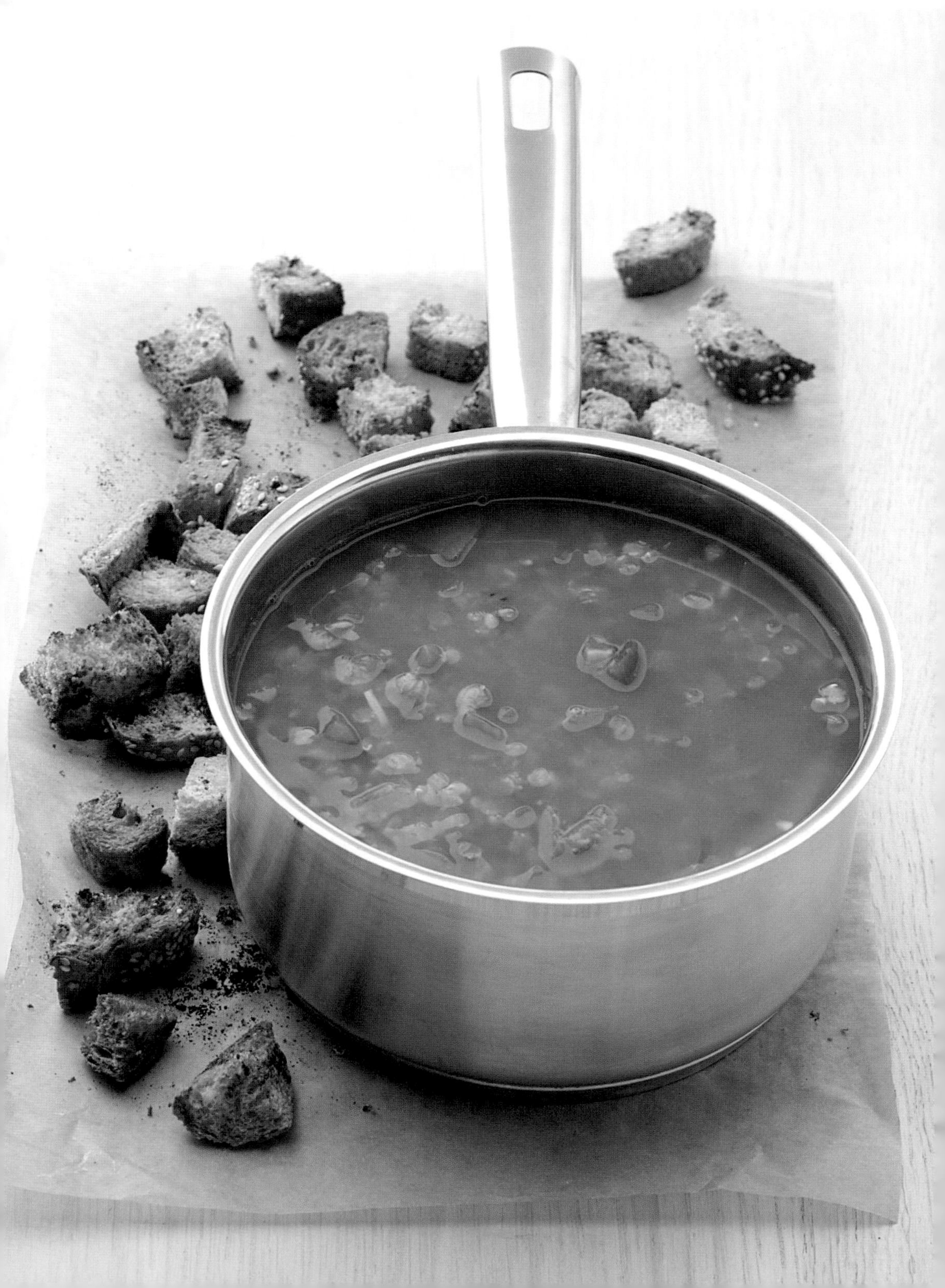

Nutritional values
Kcals 160
fat 4.8 g
saturates 1.3 g
sugars 10.8 g
salt 0.4 g

Preparation time
20 minutes
Cooking time
15 minutes
Serves
4

NUTRITIONAL TIP
While it might be tempting to add butter and a swirl of cream for those not on a low-cholesterol diet, it really isn't necessary. Don't let on, and your fellow diners will be none the wiser.

Gingered leek & watercress soup

This pretty, pale green, speckled soup is delicately flavoured with just a hint of ginger. Serve as a light lunch with some granary bread topped with cottage cheese or as a starter before a dish of grilled or steamed fish.

2 leeks, about 400 g (13 oz) in total, slit and well washed

1 tablespoon olive oil

1 potato, about 175 g (6 oz), cut into small dice

3.5 cm (1½ inch) piece of fresh root ginger, finely chopped

85 g (3¼ oz) watercress

600 ml (1 pint) low-salt vegetable stock

450 ml (14 fl oz) skimmed milk

4 tablespoons low-fat natural yogurt

pepper

1 Thickly slice the leeks, keeping the white and green slices separate.

2 Heat the oil in a medium-sized saucepan, add the white sliced leeks, potato and ginger and fry gently, stirring occasionally, for about 5 minutes or until softened but not browned.

3 Add the green leek slices, watercress, stock and a little pepper and bring the stock to the boil. Cover and simmer for 10 minutes until all the vegetables are tender and the watercress is still bright green.

4 Purée the mixture in batches in a food processor or liquidizer until smooth, then return to the pan. Stir in the milk and reheat the soup.

5 Ladle into bowls, add a tablespoon of yogurt to each and swirl lightly with a spoon.

Nutritional values

Kcals 104

fat 3.1 g

saturates 1 g

sugars 4.6 g

salt 0.7 g

Preparation time

25 minutes

Cooking time

36 minutes

Serves

6

✚ **NUTRITIONAL TIP**

Boosting your diet with foods rich in soluble fibre, such as canned kidney beans, can help to lower blood cholesterol. The fibre works its magic by binding with cholesterol and preventing it from being reabsorbed into the blood.

Red bean & spiced pumpkin soup

A warming soup, ideal for winter, is flavoured with a blend of Middle Eastern spices, including fennel, coriander and cloves, and coarsely puréed for a rougher texture. Serve with warm granary bread.

1 tablespoon sunflower oil

1 onion, finely chopped

2 garlic cloves, finely chopped (optional)

1 teaspoon fennel seeds, roughly crushed

1 teaspoon coriander seeds, roughly crushed

$1/2$ teaspoon turmeric

$1/2$ teaspoon ground ginger

$1/4$ teaspoon ground cloves

1 small pumpkin or butternut squash, about 625 g ($1^1/4$ lb), peeled, deseeded and diced

410 g ($13^1/2$ oz) can red kidney beans, drained

1.3 litres ($2^1/4$ pints) low-salt vegetable stock

pepper

small bunch of fresh coriander, to garnish

1 Heat the oil in a saucepan, add the onion and fry for 5 minutes or until softened and just beginning to brown. Stir in the garlic and spices and cook for 1 minute.

2 Add the pumpkin or butternut squash, beans, stock and a little pepper. Bring to the boil, stir well, then cover and simmer for 30 minutes.

3 Coarsely purée the soup in batches in a food processor or liquidizer so that flecks of the beans are still visible. Return to the saucepan and reheat.

4 Ladle into bowls and sprinkle over some torn coriander leaves to garnish.

Nutritional values
Kcals 258
fat 12.3 g
saturates 2.5 g
sugars 18.7 g
salt 0.9 g

Preparation time
15 minutes
Cooking time
23–24 minutes
Serves
4

NUTRITIONAL TIP
Although nuts do contain high quantities of fat, they are mainly heart-healthy unsaturated fats.

Curried cauliflower & cashew soup

Cauliflower is one of the underestimated and little used vegetables. Low in calories, it can be transformed with Indian spices into this tasty soup, which is quick and easy enough to make into a midweek lunch or smart enough to share with friends.

1 tablespoon sunflower oil

1 onion, finely chopped

4 teaspoons mild curry paste

50 g (2 oz) cashew nuts

1 cauliflower, about 500 g (1 lb) when trimmed, cut into florets

600 ml (1 pint) low-salt vegetable stock

450 ml (¾ pint) skimmed milk

pepper

To garnish
4 tablespoons low-fat natural yogurt

4 teaspoons mango chutney

1 Heat the oil in a medium-sized saucepan, add the onion and fry for 5 minutes or until softened and just beginning to colour. Add the curry paste and three-quarters of the nuts and fry for 1 minute.

2 Reserve a few tiny cauliflower florets for garnish and add the rest to the pan with the stock and a little pepper. Bring to the boil, stir well, then cover and simmer for 15 minutes or until the cauliflower is just tender.

3 Purée the soup in batches in a liquidizer or food processor and return to the saucepan. Stir in the milk and reheat gently.

4 Dry-fry the remaining nuts and reserved cauliflower florets for 2–3 minutes or until they are tinged with brown.

5 Ladle the soup into bowls, swirl in the yogurt and chutney, then float the toasted cauliflower and cashews on top.

Nutritional values

Kcals 199

fat 6.6 g

saturates 1.4 g

sugars 11.3 g

salt 0.9 g

Preparation time

30 minutes

Cooking time

53–55 minutes

Serves

4

NUTRITIONAL TIP

Aubergines are usually fried in lots of oil before being added to soups or casseroles. Grilling them whole adds flavour and cuts out the need for oil.

Smoked aubergine soup

This light, fresh-tasting soup is made by grilling, rather than frying, the aubergine for maximum flavour, then simmering it with mushrooms, onions and lemons. This Greek-inspired soup is topped off with dainty toasted olive croutons.

1 aubergine, about 300 g (10 oz) in total

1 tablespoon olive oil

1 onion, finely chopped

250 g (8 oz) closed-cup mushrooms, sliced

2 garlic cloves, finely chopped

25 g (1 oz) long grain white rice

600 ml (1 pint) low-salt vegetable stock

600 ml (1 pint) skimmed milk

grated rind of 1 lemon, the rest of the lemon cut into wedges

pepper

To serve
4 slices from a wholemeal torpedo roll or French stick, about 65 g (2½ oz) in total

25 g (1 oz) pitted black olives

small sprig of rosemary (optional)

1 teaspoon olive oil

1 Prick the end of the aubergine, just beneath the stalk, 2–3 times with a fork. Cook under a preheated grill for 20–25 minutes, turning several times until the skin is charred and blackened and the centre is softened. Transfer to a chopping board and leave to cool slightly.

2 Heat the oil in a medium-sized saucepan, add the onion and fry gently for 5 minutes or until just beginning to turn golden. Stir in the mushrooms and garlic and fry for 3 minutes. Stir in the rice, stock and a little pepper and bring to the boil.

3 Meanwhile, cut the aubergine in half and use a spoon to scoop the soft flesh away from the blackened skin and stalk. Roughly chop the flesh, then stir it into the stock.

4 Cover the pan and simmer for 30 minutes. Cool slightly, then purée in batches in a food processor or liquidizer until smooth. Return to the pan, stir in the milk and lemon rind and reheat gently.

5 Toast the bread. Finely chop the olives with the rosemary (if used). Mix with the oil and a little pepper and spread on the toast.

6 Ladle the soup into bowls and add a slice of toast. Serve lemon wedges separately so that diners can add it to taste.

Nutritional values

Kcals 397

fat 8.9 g

saturates 3.5 g

sugars 9.1 g

salt 0.8 g

Preparation time

15 minutes

Cooking time

20 minutes

Serves

4

NUTRITIONAL TIP

Using extra-lean minced beef slashes the fat content of this dish. A 100 g (3½ oz) serving of regular mince contains 16.2 g fat and 7.1 g saturates, whereas the same serving of extra-lean mince contains just 9.6 g fat and 4.2 g saturates.

Mexican beef wraps

Fed up with sandwiches for lunch? Try these meaty wraps filled with chilli-, paprika- and cumin-spiced, extra-lean minced beef topped with fresh-tasting natural yogurt and a coriander-speckled salad.

300 g (10 oz) extra-lean minced beef

1 onion, finely chopped

1 teaspoon cumin seeds, roughly crushed

1 teaspoon paprika

½–1 teaspoon chilli powder, to taste

8 soft flour tortillas 320 g (10½ oz)

200 g (7 oz) low-fat natural yogurt

½ small iceberg lettuce, shredded

2 tomatoes, diced

small bunch of fresh coriander leaves, roughly chopped

1 Dry-fry the mince and onion in a nonstick frying pan for 10 minutes over a medium to low heat, stirring and breaking up the mince with a wooden spoon until it is evenly browned.

2 Stir in the cumin and ground spices and cook for 10 more minutes until the mince is cooked through.

3 Warm the tortillas according to the instructions on the packet. Separate and divide the mince among them. Top with spoonfuls of the yogurt, lettuce, tomatoes and coriander. Roll up tightly and serve at once.

Nutritional values	Preparation time	+ NUTRITIONAL TIP
Kcals 199	15 minutes	It is important to reduce saturated fats,
fat 7.1 g	**Cooking time**	but the healthy monounsaturated fats
saturates 1.9 g	3 minutes	found in olive oil and omega-3 fatty acids
sugars 4.3 g	**Serves**	found in oily fish are needed by the body
salt 0.5 g	4	for a healthy heart and good circulation.

Sardine & lentil salad

This tasty salad can be enjoyed at home or, if the weather is good, pack up the sardine mixture in a plastic container and the leaves into a plastic bag or separate box and mix them together at your picnic destination.

100 g (3½ oz) frozen peas

2 x 120 g (3¾ oz) cans boneless, skinless sardines in tomato sauce

410 g (13½ oz) can green lentils, rinsed and drained

5 cm (2 inch) piece of cucumber, diced

1 small red onion, chopped

small bunch of mint

grated rind and juice of 1 lemon

1 cos lettuce, leaves separated

pepper

1 Cook the peas in a saucepan of boiling water for 3 minutes. Alternatively, cook them in the microwave for 1½ minutes on full power.

2 Flake the sardines into chunks and put them in a large salad bowl with their sauce. Add the lentils, drained peas, cucumber and onion. Roughly tear the mint into pieces and add to the salad with the lemon rind and juice and a little pepper and toss together.

3 Arrange the lettuce leaves on serving plates and spoon the sardine salad on top.

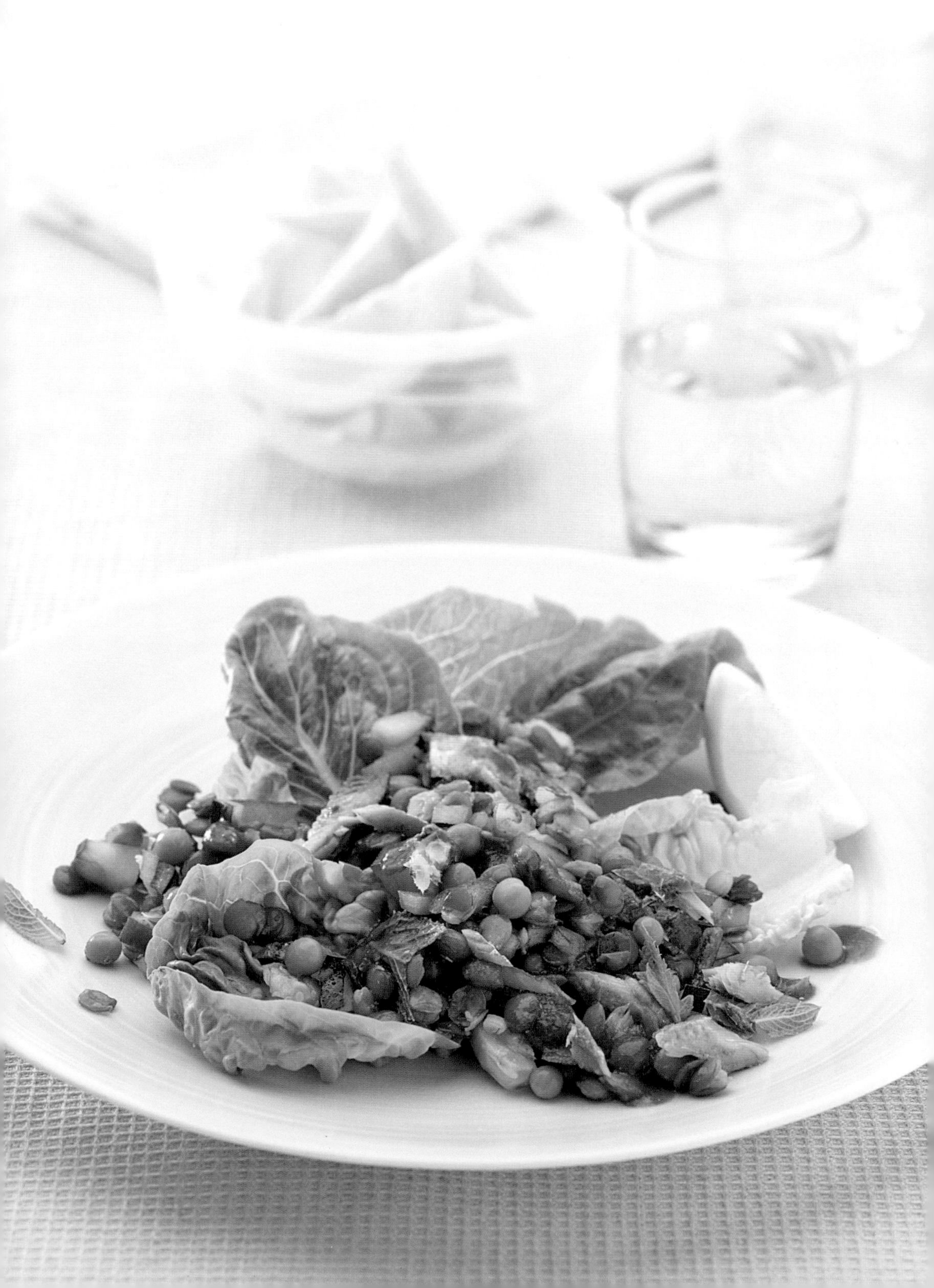

Nutritional values
Kcals 344
fat 13.5 g
saturates 2.5 g
sugars 9.3 g
salt 1 g
fibre

Preparation time
20 minutes
Cooking time
10 minutes
Serves
4

NUTRITIONAL TIP
Both olive oil and avocados have a high content of monounsaturated fatty acids, which help reduce LDL or 'bad' cholesterol while maintaining levels of HDL or 'good' cholesterol.

Avocado & chilli hummus

This moreish dip mixes avocado with chickpeas, toasted sesame seeds and yogurt with a hint of chilli. You may like to serve this with peppery radishes, cherry tomatoes or fingers of toast, or spread into wholegrain rolls and finished with green salad leaves.

2 tablespoons sesame seeds

1 red chilli, deseeded and finely chopped

410 g (13½ oz) can chickpeas, drained

1 ripe avocado, halved, stoned and peeled

juice of 1 lemon

2 garlic cloves, finely chopped

100 g (3½ oz) low-fat natural yogurt

pepper

little paprika, to garnish

To serve
4 wholemeal pittas, toasted

1 red pepper, cored, deseeded and cut into strips

¼ cucumber, cut into sticks

1 large carrot, cut into sticks

1 Dry-fry the sesame seeds in a frying pan until they are just beginning to brown. Tip into a liquidizer or food processor, add the chilli and chickpeas and blend together.

2 Add the avocado flesh to the chickpeas with the lemon juice, garlic, yogurt and a little pepper. Blend to make a smooth purée.

3 Spoon the hummus into a shallow dish set on a large plate and sprinkle over a little paprika.

4 Grill the pittas or dry-fry in a preheated ridged frying pan, until hot and puffy. Cut them into strips and arrange them around the hummus with the other vegetable dippers. Serve within 30 minutes of making or the avocado will discolour.

Nutritional values

Kcals 225

fat 14.7 g

saturates 3 g

sugars 19.5 g

salt 0.2 g

fibre

Preparation time

20 minutes,

plus marinating

Serves

4

NUTRITIONAL TIP

Both tomatoes and ruby grapefruit contain good amounts of lycopene, an antioxidant that has been linked to keeping the heart healthy.

Summer avocado & melon salad

This chunky, refreshing blend of melon, tomatoes, cucumber and avocado is dotted with chopped coriander, although if you have mint growing in the garden you may prefer to add a little of this.

1 ruby grapefruit

1 galia melon, halved, deseeded and peeled

¼ cucumber

3 tomatoes

small bunch of fresh coriander, roughly chopped

2 avocados

1 Use a small serrated knife to cut a slice off the top and bottom of the grapefruit, then cut the peel away from the sides. Hold the grapefruit over a bowl and cut through the membrane to release the segments. Squeeze the juice from the membrane.

2 Cut the melon into large dice and the cucumber and tomatoes into smaller dice. Add these to the grapefruit with the coriander and toss together. Set aside for 30 minutes for the flavours to develop.

3 Just before serving, cut the avocados in half and remove the stones. Peel and dice the flesh, add it to the salad and toss together. Spoon into shallow dishes and serve.

Nutritional values

Kcals 298

fat 10.5 g

saturates 1.6 g

sugars 5 g

salt 0.5 g

Preparation time

15 minutes

Cooking time

12 minutes

Serves

4

NUTRITIONAL TIP

Only fresh tuna counts as an oil-rich fish because processing and canning tuna destroys omega-3 fats. Canned tuna still counts towards your two weekly servings of fish.

Tuna pasta salad

Quick and easy to put together, this hearty salad travels well, so is ideal for packed lunches or to take on family picnics. Choose tuna canned in spring water rather than oil or brine.

175 g (6 oz) wholewheat pasta shapes

100 g (3½ oz) frozen sweetcorn

3 tablespoons olive oil

juice of 1 lemon

1 teaspoon tomato purée

1–2 garlic cloves, finely chopped (optional)

small bunch of basil, torn

200 g (7 oz) can tuna in spring water, drained and flaked

3 tomatoes, about 200 g (7 oz) in total, diced

1 green pepper, cored, deseeded and diced

pepper

1 Bring a saucepan of water to the boil, add the pasta and cook for 8 minutes. Add the sweetcorn and cook for 2 more minutes until the pasta is tender.

2 Meanwhile, make the dressing by mixing together the oil, lemon juice, tomato purée, garlic (if used) and basil in a salad bowl. Season with pepper. Drain the pasta and mix into the dressing until evenly coated.

3 Stir in the tuna, tomatoes and green pepper, then spoon the salad into bowls to serve.

Nutritional values

Kcals 399

fat 20.7 g

saturates 4 g

sugars 13.3 g

salt 1.3 g

Preparation time

15 minutes

Serves

4

NUTRITIONAL TIP

Don't be tempted to add any oil: the couscous grains are light and separate enough without it.

Curried couscous salad

If you get fed up with sandwiches snatched at your desk, make up this tasty salad the night before, store it in the refrigerator in individual plastic boxes and take one to work in a mini insulated bag.

juice of 1 orange

2 teaspoons mild curry paste

200 g (7 oz) couscous

50 g (2 oz) sultanas

300 ml (½ pint) boiling water

250 g (8 oz) smoked mackerel fillets

1 small red onion, finely chopped

½ red pepper, cored, deseeded and diced

2 tomatoes, diced

small bunch of fresh coriander, roughly chopped

pepper

1 Put the orange juice and curry paste into a medium-sized bowl and fork together. Add the couscous, sultanas and a little pepper, then add the boiling water and fork together. Leave to stand for 5 minutes.

2 Peel the skin off the mackerel fillets and break the flesh into large flakes, discarding any bones.

3 Add the mackerel, onion, red pepper and tomatoes to the couscous and mix together lightly. Sprinkle the coriander over the top, then spoon on to plates.

Nutritional values

Kcals 282

fat 3.5 g

saturates 1.1 g

sugars 7.2 g

salt 1.2 g

fibre

Preparation time

15 minutes

Cooking time

5 minutes

Serves

4

NUTRITIONAL TIP

To keep your fat intake low, remove the skin from chicken before you cook it. That way, the extra fat from the skin won't melt into the meat – and you won't be tempted to eat it!

Seared chicken sandwich

Briefly tossing pieces of chicken in balsamic vinegar is a good way of adding flavour without using salt.

250 g (8 oz) mini chicken breast fillets

8 teaspoons balsamic vinegar

8 slices of granary bread

6 tablespoons low-fat natural yogurt

¹/₂–1 teaspoon freshly grated hot horseradish or horseradish sauce, to taste

100 g (3¹/₂ oz) mixed salad leaves with beetroot strips

pepper

1 Put the chicken fillets into a plastic bag with half the vinegar and toss together until evenly coated.

2 Heat a nonstick frying pan, lift the chicken out of the plastic bag with a fork and add the pieces to the pan. Fry for 3 minutes, turn and drizzle with the vinegar from the bag and cook for 2 more minutes or until browned and cooked through.

3 Toast the bread lightly on both sides. Slice the chicken into long thin strips and arrange them on 4 slices of toast. Mix together the yogurt and horseradish and a little pepper to taste. Add the salad leaves and toss together.

4 Spoon the yogurt and salad leaves over the chicken, drizzle over the remaining vinegar, if liked, and top with the remaining toast. Cut each sandwich in half and serve immediately.

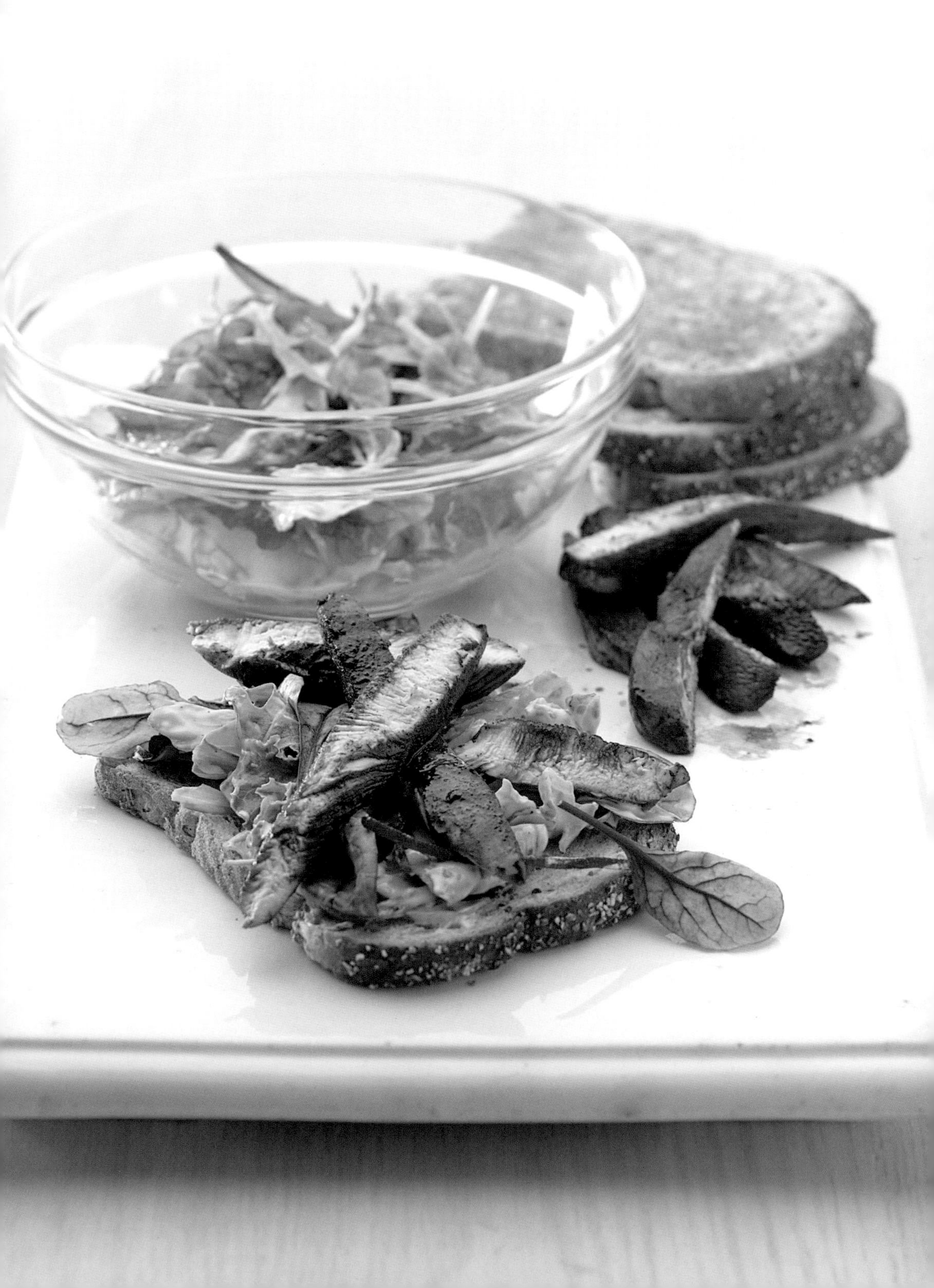

Nutritional values	Preparation time	✚ NUTRITIONAL TIP
Kcals 142	15 minutes	Pomegranates are a rich source of
fat 1.6 g	**Cooking time**	antioxidants, particularly polyphenols, which
saturates 0.7 g	4 minutes	research shows may help to reduce LDL or
sugars 11.1 g	**Serves**	'bad' cholesterol. In addition, they also
salt 0.8 g	4	contain antioxidant vitamins A, C and E.

Cheesy toasties with raspberry salad

Adding a few fresh raspberries and some jewelled ruby pomegranate seeds transforms a simple salad into an exotic light lunch topped with cottage cheese toasts.

125 g (4 oz) mixed salad leaves, including baby red chard leaves

½ red onion, thinly sliced

100 g (3½ oz) fresh raspberries

2 tablespoons balsamic vinegar

1 pomegranate

8 slices, about 75 g (3 oz), wholewheat French bread

250 g (8 oz) low-fat cottage cheese

little paprika

1 Put the salad leaves in a bowl with the onion and raspberries. Drizzle with the vinegar and toss together lightly.

2 Cut the pomegranate into quarters, flex the skin and pop out the seeds. Sprinkle half the seeds over the salad, then transfer the salad to 4 serving plates.

3 Toast the bread on both sides and arrange a slice in the centre of each serving plate. Mix the remaining pomegranate seeds into the cottage cheese, spoon on to the toast and serve sprinkled with a little paprika.

suppers

Nutritional values

Kcals 400

fat 3.4 g

saturates 0.9 g

sugars 15 g

salt 0.3 g

Preparation time

30 minutes, plus

marinating

Cooking time

35–42 minutes

Serves

4

+ NUTRITIONAL TIP

Marinades don't have to be made with oil. This version uses canned fruit juice, although fresh orange, lemon or lime juice could be mixed with spices and other flavourings. Skinless chicken breasts or diced tofu could be used as an alternative to the turkey.

Caribbean turkey skewers with salsa

Fresh, fruity and full of Caribbean sunshine, these summery turkey skewers are flavoured with pineapple juice and spices and served with a pineapple, tomato and sweetcorn salsa spiked with chilli, ginger and fresh coriander.

220 g (7½ oz) can pineapple rings in natural juice

1 tablespoon tomato ketchup

1 teaspoon paprika

½ teaspoon ground cinnamon

large pinch of ground allspice

4 boneless, skinless turkey breast steaks, about 500 g (1 lb) in total, cubed

2 tomatoes, diced

100 g (3½ oz) frozen sweetcorn, just thawed

½ red chilli, deseeded and finely chopped (optional)

1.5 cm (¾ inch) piece of fresh root ginger, finely chopped

small bunch of fresh coriander, roughly chopped

200 g (7 oz) easy-cook brown rice

1 red pepper, cored, deseeded and cut into chunks

1 orange pepper, cored, deseeded and cut into chunks

1 Drain the pineapple and put 4 tablespoons of the juice into a bowl. Stir the ketchup and spices into the measured juice, add the turkey pieces and toss together. Leave to marinate for at least 30 minutes.

2 Meanwhile, make the salsa. Finely chop the pineapple rings and put in a bowl with the tomatoes and sweetcorn. Add the chilli (if used), ginger and half the coriander and toss together.

3 Put the brown rice in a saucepan of boiling water and cook for 25–30 minutes or until tender.

4 Thread the pepper chunks on to 12 wooden or metal skewers, then thread the turkey above the peppers. Sprinkle with the remaining chopped coriander. Grill the skewers under a preheated hot grill for 10–12 minutes, turning several times until well browned and the turkey is cooked through.

5 Drain the rice and spoon on to plates, top with the skewers and serve with spoonfuls of the salsa

Nutritional values

Kcals 435

fat 20.6 g

saturates 5.7 g

sugars 15.1 g

salt 0.4 g

Preparation time

30 minutes

Cooking time

about 1 hour 20 minutes

Serves

4

NUTRITIONAL TIP

When you are cooking a whole chicken, always remove any fat you can see beneath the skin. You'll often find excess fat around the neck: simply trim this off and throw it away

Maple roasted chicken

A simple homely roast is made with all the vegetables cooked alongside the chicken. Rather than adding lots of oil to the potatoes, they are roasted with cider and bay leaves and glazed with maple syrup.

1.3 kg (2 lb 10 oz) oven-ready chicken, rinsed and drained

4 bay leaves

2 onions, cut into wedges

2 Cox's apples, cored and quartered

2 parsnips, about 325 g (11 oz) in total, cut into thin wedges

400 g (13 oz) new potatoes, scrubbed and halved if large

300 ml (½ pint) dry cider

4 teaspoons maple syrup

300 ml (½ pint) low-salt vegetable stock

few drops of gravy browning (optional)

pepper

1 Put the chicken on a wire rack in a roasting tin, tuck 2 bay leaves into the body cavity and sprinkle with a little pepper. Cover the top loosely with foil and bake in a preheated oven, 190°C (375°F), Gas Mark 5, for 40 minutes.

2 Remove the rack and pour away any fat from the chicken. Add the onion, apples, parsnips, potatoes and remaining bay leaves to the roasting tin. Pour in the cider, drizzle the maple syrup over the top and sprinkle with a little more pepper. Roast for 30–40 minutes until the vegetables and chicken are golden and the juices run clear when the thickest parts of the chicken leg and breast are pierced with a skewer.

3 Transfer the chicken and vegetables on to a serving dish. Add the stock to the roasting tin, bring to the boil and cook for 3–4 minutes. Stir in a few drops of gravy browning (if used), then strain into a jug to serve.

Nutritional values

Kcals 306

fat 7 g

saturates 1.4 g

sugars 9.7 g

salt 0.5 g

Preparation time

20 minutes

Cooking time

about 2¼ hours

Serves

4

NUTRITIONAL TIP

Most of the fat in chicken is found in the skin, so always remove it before casseroling.

Stoved chicken

All the ingredients of this Scottish-style dish are traditionally cooked together in one pot. The secret of success lies in long, slow cooking, so don't worry if you get a little delayed before removing the lid for the last 30 minutes of cooking.

4 large skinless chicken thighs, about 625 g (1¼ lb) in total

1 tablespoon sunflower oil

1 small leek, about 150 g (5 oz), slit, rinsed and sliced

1 tablespoon plain flour

450 ml (¾ pint) low-salt vegetable stock

1 teaspoon English mustard

200 g (7 oz) carrot, diced

175 g (6 oz) swede, diced

150 g (5 oz) parsnip, diced

2–3 stems rosemary

500 g (1 lb) potatoes, thinly sliced

pepper

1 Rinse the chicken in cold water, drain well and cut away the skin. Heat the oil in a frying pan, add the chicken and fry over a high heat for 5 minutes, turning until evenly browned.

2 Transfer the chicken pieces to a 2.5 litre (4 pint) casserole dish. Add the leek to the frying pan and cook gently for 5 minutes or until softened and just beginning to brown.

3 Stir in the flour, then gradually mix in the stock, mustard and a little pepper and bring to the boil.

4 Add the diced vegetables to the casserole dish with the rosemary. Pour the hot stock over them and arrange the potatoes on top, overlapping the slices slightly and pressing them beneath the stock. Cover and bake in a preheated oven, 160°C (325°F), Gas Mark 3, for 1½ hours.

5 Remove the lid and cook for 30 minutes more or until the potatoes are browned. Serve in shallow bowls with steamed green beans or broccoli.

Nutritional values
Kcals 410
fat 3.7 g
saturates 1.1 g
sugars 8.1 g
salt 0.3 g

Preparation time
10 minutes
Cooking time
20 minutes
Serves
4

+ NUTRITIONAL TIP
Small amounts of red wine have been linked to reducing heart disease, but only in men over 40 and postmenopausal women. In particular, red wine has received a lot of attention because it contains heart-healthy flavonoids.

Chicken cacciatore

Think of pasta dishes and you tend to think of sauces bathed in lots of olive oil or rich buttery sauces. This version roasts low-fat chicken breasts with tiny tomatoes and red onion wedges in a rich red wine and balsamic vinegar sauce.

4 boneless, skinless chicken breasts, each about 125 g (4 oz)

500 g (1 lb) cherry or mini plum tomatoes, halved

1 red onion, cut into wedges

2 garlic cloves, finely chopped

2–3 stems rosemary, torn into pieces

6 tablespoons red wine

2 tablespoons balsamic vinegar

250 g (8 oz) dried linguine or fettuccine

2 tablespoons grated fat-reduced mature Cheddar cheese (optional)

pepper

1 Put the chicken breasts into a colander, rinse with cold water and drain well. Transfer the chicken into a large roasting tin or ovenproof dish so that the chicken is in a single layer. Add the tomatoes and onion, then sprinkle over the garlic and rosemary. Drizzle with the wine and vinegar and add a little pepper.

2 Bake in a preheated oven, 220°C (425°F), Gas Mark 7, for 20 minutes or until the onions and chicken are browned and the juices run clear when the chicken is pierced with a skewer.

3 Halfway through cooking, bring a large saucepan of water to the boil, add the pasta and cook for 8–10 minutes until just tender.

4 Drain the pasta and return to the empty pan. Slice the chicken breasts and add to the pasta with the onions, tomatoes and pan juices. Toss together and spoon into bowls. Sprinkle with a little rosemary and top with cheese, if liked.

Nutritional values

Kcals 381

fat 8.6 g

saturates 2.8 g

sugars 8.4 g

salt 0.5 g

Preparation time

20 minutes

Cooking time

about 2¼ hours

Serves

4

+ NUTRITIONAL TIP

Barley is a good source of soluble fibre, which helps not only to lower cholesterol but also to keep blood sugar levels steady, so that we're less likely to feel hungry between meals and resort to fatty and sugary snacks.

Beef & barley casserole

Slowly baked with red wine and garlic, this comforting beef supper dish is packed with fibre. It's perfect served with baby Brussels sprouts and mashed swede. Instead of using garlic and red wine, you could try adding some beer or extra stock.

1 tablespoon olive oil

500 g (1 lb) lean diced stewing beef, any fat trimmed away

1 onion, chopped

2 garlic cloves, finely chopped

1 tablespoon plain flour

200 ml (7 fl oz) red wine

900 ml (1½ pints) low-salt vegetable stock

100 g (3½ oz) pearl barley

300 g (10 oz) carrots, cut into chunks

1 tablespoon tomato purée

1 bouquet garni

pepper

1 Heat the oil in a flameproof casserole, add the beef a few pieces at a time, then stir in the onion and fry over a high heat for 5 minutes or until evenly browned. Stir in the garlic and cook for 1 minute.

2 Stir in the flour, then mix in the wine and 600 ml (1 pint) stock. Add the pearl barley, carrots, tomato purée, bouquet garni and a little pepper and mix well.

3 Add the lid and cook in a preheated oven, 180°C (350°F), Gas Mark 4, for 2 hours until the beef and barley are tender and much of the stock has been absorbed by the barley. Check 30 minutes before the end of cooking, stir and mix in the remaining stock to taste.

4 Spoon into shallow bowls and serve as it is, or with steamed baby Brussels sprouts or green beans and mashed swede.

Nutritional values

Kcals 450

fat 21.6 g

saturates 8.1 g

sugars 15.9 g

salt 1.3 g

Preparation time

45 minutes

Cooking time

about 1 hour

10 minutes

Serves

4

+ NUTRITIONAL TIP

Using skimmed milk and cornflour to make a white sauce, rather than making a traditional roux sauce with flour, butter and full-fat milk, is not only easier but also slashes the fat and saturates content of the sauce.

Lasagne

There is no need to strike this Italian favourite off the menu, especially if low-fat or reduced-fat ingredients are boosted with lots of peppers and courgettes. Serve with a green salad tossed with balsamic vinegar or lemon juice.

9 lasagne sheets, 175 g (6 oz)

Meat sauce
2 teaspoons olive oil

300 g (10 oz) extra-lean minced beef

1 onion, chopped

1½ peppers, cored, deseeded and diced

125 g (4 oz) courgette, diced

2 garlic cloves, finely chopped

400 g (13 oz) can chopped tomatoes

200 ml (7 fl oz) low-salt vegetable stock

few sprigs of oregano or basil

pepper

Cheese sauce
40 g (1½ oz) cornflour

450 ml (¾ pint) skimmed milk

1 teaspoon Dijon mustard

little grated nutmeg

75 g (3 oz) low-fat mature cheese

1 Heat the oil in a saucepan, add the mince and onion and fry for 5 minutes, stirring and breaking up the mince with a wooden spoon until it is evenly browned.

2 Stir in the peppers, courgette and garlic and cook for 3 minutes, then mix in the canned tomatoes, stock, torn herbs and pepper. Cover and simmer for 30 minutes, stirring occasionally.

3 Meanwhile, make the cheese sauce. Put the cornflour into a small bowl and mix with a little of the milk to make a smooth paste. Pour into a saucepan and mix in the remaining milk, mustard, nutmeg and a little pepper. Bring to the boil, whisking until thickened and smooth. Grate the cheese and stir three-quarters of it into the sauce.

4 Spoon a thin layer of the meat mixture into the base of a 20 cm (8 inch) square, 5 cm (2 inches) deep ovenproof dish. Cover with 3 sheets of lasagne then half the mince mixture. Cover with 3 more sheets of lasagne, then half the cheese sauce and the remaining meat sauce. Top with the remaining lasagne sheets and the cheese sauce.

5 Bake in a preheated oven, 180°C (350°F), Gas Mark 4, for 30–35 minutes until the top is golden and the pasta tender.

Nutritional values
Kcals 437
fat 15.4 g
saturates 4.9 g
sugars 2.8 g
salt 0.5 g

Preparation time
15 minutes
Cooking time
about 30 minutes
Serves
4

NUTRITIONAL TIP
Always trim off all the visible fat from steaks before cooking. Egg white is virtually fat free and when mixed with just a tiny amount of oil produces golden chips that look just like deep-fried ones.

Seared steak with mustardy chips

Being on a low-cholesterol diet doesn't mean that you have to give up all your favourite foods, just that you may need to rethink the way in which you cook them, as this juicy steak with all the trimmings proves.

500 g (1 lb) potatoes, scrubbed

2 tablespoons olive oil

1 egg white

1 teaspoon wholegrain mustard

$\frac{1}{2}$ teaspoon turmeric

250 g (8 oz) cherry tomatoes on the vine

250 g (8 oz) cup mushrooms

4 thick-cut sirloin steaks, each 200 g (7 oz), fat trimmed away

pepper

To serve
green salad

1 Cut the potatoes in half lengthways, then into chunky wedges. Put 1 tablespoon oil in a bowl, add the egg white, mustard, turmeric and a little pepper and fork together until the egg white is slightly frothy. Add the potatoes and toss together.

2 Arrange the potatoes in a single layer on a lightly oiled baking sheet and cook in a preheated oven, 230°C (450°F), Gas Mark 8, for 10 minutes. Add the tomatoes and cook for 5 more minutes or until the chips are golden and the tomato skins just beginning to split. Turn off the oven.

3 Brush the mushrooms with the remaining oil. Sprinkle the steak with a little pepper. Preheat a nonstick ridged or ordinary frying pan, add the steak and mushrooms and cook the steak for 1½–2 minutes each side for rare, 3 4 minutes each side for medium and 5–6 minutes each side for well done, or to taste.

4 Transfer the steak, chips and vegetables to serving plates and serve with a green salad dressed with a little lemon juice or balsamic vinegar.

Nutritional values

Kcals 372

fat 10.7 g

saturates 4.4 g

sugars 8 g

salt 0.3 g

Preparation time

30 minutes

Cooking time

30 minutes

Serves

4

NUTRITIONAL TIP

Bulgar wheat makes a tasty, low-fat alternative to pasta, rice or couscous and is a good source of fibre.

Spiced meatballs with bulgar salad

Oven-baked mini meatballs are given a Middle Eastern twist. They are flavoured with lemon and allspice and served on a bulgar wheat salad flecked with fresh chopped fragrant mint and parsley leaves and drizzled with a garlicky tomato sauce.

750 ml (1¼ pints) water

175 g (6 oz) bulgar wheat

400 g (13 oz) extra-lean minced beef

½ onion, finely chopped

grated rind and juice of 1 lemon

¼ teaspoon ground allspice

3 tablespoons chopped mint, plus extra leaves to garnish (optional)

3 tablespoons chopped parsley, plus extra leaves to garnish (optional)

pepper

Tomato sauce
1 onion, chopped

2 garlic cloves, finely chopped

400 g (13 oz) fresh tomatoes, skinned (if liked) and diced

2 teaspoons tomato purée

1 Put the water in a medium-sized saucepan, bring to the boil, add the bulgar wheat and simmer for 10 minutes until just tender. Drain and reserve.

2 Put the meat in a bowl, add the onion, lemon rind, allspice and pepper. Add 6 tablespoons of the cooked bulgar, mix together and shape into 24 small balls.

3 Put the meatballs into a nonstick roasting tin and cook in a preheated oven, 180°C (350°F), Gas Mark 4, for 20 minutes, turning once, until evenly browned and cooked through.

4 Meanwhile, make the tomato sauce. Put the onion, garlic, tomatoes, tomato purée and a little pepper into a saucepan, cover and simmer for 20 minutes, stirring occasionally, until softened. Purée until smooth, then reheat.

5 Stir the lemon juice into the remaining bulgar wheat and reheat it gently. Mix in the chopped herbs and a little pepper and spoon it on to plates. Stir the meatballs into the tomato sauce, spoon over the bulgar and garnish with a few extra herb leaves, if liked.

Nutritional values

Kcals 464

fat 12.9 g

saturates 4.6 g

sugars 20.3 g

salt 0.5 g

Preparation time

15 minutes

Cooking time

37–42 minutes

Serves

4

NUTRITIONAL TIP

Lamb contains more fat than beef or pork, so remove any before cooking. Leg steaks are leaner cuts – 100 g (3½ oz) grilled leg steaks contain 9 g fat and 3.6 g saturates, while grilled neck cutlets have 13.8 g fat and 6.5 g saturates in 100 g (3½ oz).

Lamb pilaf

This easy, one-pan supper dish is made with a base of brown rice flavoured with allspice, cinnamon and garlic. Although lamb is high in fat, using lean leg steaks and mixing the meat with mushrooms means a little goes a long way.

1 tablespoon olive oil

350 g (11½ oz) lamb leg steaks, fat trimmed off and meat diced

1 onion, chopped

200 g (7 oz) cup mushrooms, quartered

2 garlic cloves, finely chopped

200 g (7 oz) long grain brown rice

½ teaspoon ground allspice

½ teaspoon ground cinnamon

3 cloves, roughly crushed

75 g (3 oz) sultanas or raisins

1 litre (1¾ pints) low-salt vegetable stock

pepper

To serve
150 g (5 oz) fat-free Greek yogurt

2 tomatoes, diced

½ small red onion, finely chopped

small bunch of mint

1 Heat the oil in a nonstick frying pan, add the lamb and onion and fry, stirring, for 5 minutes or until the lamb has browned. Stir in the mushrooms and garlic and fry for 2 minutes.

2 Mix in the rice, spices, dried fruit, 600 ml (1 pint) stock and pepper. Bring to the boil, cover and simmer for 30–35 minutes, topping up with the remaining stock as needed until the rice is tender.

3 Spoon the pilaf into bowls and serve topped with spoonfuls of yogurt, tomato, onion and torn mint leaves.

Nutritional values

Kcals 387

fat 11.2 g

saturates 3.4 g

sugars 16.1 g

salt 1.2 g

Preparation time

25 minutes

Cooking time

50–55 minutes

Serves

4

NUTRITIONAL TIP

Mixing minced beef with lentils and vegetables will help to reduce the fat content without making the portions seem mean and small. In addition, lentils will help to boost your intake of soluble fibre.

Cottage pie with parsnip mash

Popular with all ages, this comforting family supper mixes lean minced beef with lots of vegetables and lentils for generously sized portions. You can make this dish earlier in the day and reheat it at 190°C (375°F), Gas Mark 5, for 35–40 minutes.

3 teaspoons sunflower oil

250 g (8 oz) extra-lean minced beef

1 onion, finely chopped

125 g (4 oz) carrot, diced

125 g (4 oz) swede, diced

65 g (2½ oz) puy lentils

200 g (7 oz) can low-salt baked beans

450 ml (¾ pint) low-salt vegetable stock

2 tablespoons Worcestershire sauce

1 tablespoon tomato purée

3 teaspoons wholegrain mustard

400 g (13 oz) parsnips, cut into chunks

250 g (8 oz) potatoes, cut into chunks

2 tablespoons fat-free fromage frais

pepper

1 Heat 2 teaspoons oil in a frying pan, add the mince and onion and fry, stirring, for 5 minutes or until the mince is evenly browned.

2 Stir in the carrot, swede and lentils, then mix in the baked beans, stock, Worcestershire sauce and tomato purée. Add 1 teaspoon mustard and a little pepper. Bring to the boil, stir well, then cover and simmer, stirring occasionally, for 45–50 minutes or until the lentils are tender and the stock has reduced and thickened.

3 Meanwhile, cook the parsnips and potatoes in a saucepan of boiling water for 20 minutes. Drain, tip them back into the pan and mash with the remaining mustard, the fromage frais and a little pepper.

4 Spoon the mince mixture into a 1.2 litre (2 pint) pie dish and top it with spoonfuls of the mash. Drizzle the top of the mash with the remaining oil and grill until browned. Serve with peas.

Nutritional values

Kcals 383

fat 8.3 g

saturates 0.8 g

sugars 12.5 g

salt 0 g

Preparation time

15 minutes

Cooking time

30 minutes

Serves

4

╋ NUTRITIONAL TIP

Pork is one of the leanest meats you can buy, with lean cuts containing as little as 4 per cent fat. Furthermore, over half the fat is heart-healthy monounsaturates and polyunsaturates.

Speedy pork stir-fry

Buying pre-prepared stir-fry vegetables saves time and can be a real help if you get back from work late. Put the rice on as soon as you can and forget about it for 20 minutes, then quickly stir-fry the pork at the last minute.

200 g (7 oz) long grain brown rice

1 tablespoon sunflower oil

400 g (13 oz) pork tenderloin, thinly sliced, large slices halved crossways

2 garlic cloves, finely chopped

300 g (10 oz) ready-prepared stir-fry vegetables

350 ml (12 fl oz) pressed apple juice

2 teaspoons tomato purée

1 teaspoon ground five spice powder

1 Bring a saucepan of water to the boil, add the rice and simmer for 30 minutes.

2 When the rice is almost cooked, heat the oil in a wok or nonstick frying pan, add the pork and garlic and fry, stirring, over a high heat for 3 minutes.

3 Add the prepared vegetables and stir-fry for 3 minutes. Mix the apple juice with the tomato purée and spice powder, pour the mixture into the pan and cook for 1 minute.

4 Drain the rice, spoon it into serving bowls and top with the pork stir-fry.

Nutritional values
Kcals 546
fat 13.7 g
saturates 4.6 g
sugars 19.9 g
salt 0.5 g

Preparation time
25 minutes
Cooking time
1 hour 36 minutes
Serves
4

+ NUTRITIONAL TIP
Using lots of different spices to flavour food means you don't need to add salt, large amounts of which can cause high blood pressure, which, in turn, is a risk factor for heart disease.

Lamb tagine with saffron couscous

Don't be put off by the long list of ingredients: this dish is really easy and quick to put together. Once it is in the oven you can forget about it, and if you get delayed by 15–30 minutes it won't come to any harm – just top up with a little extra stock if necessary.

400 g (13 oz) lamb rump steaks

1 tablespoon olive oil

1 onion, chopped

2 garlic cloves, finely chopped

6 cloves

1 teaspoon ground cinnamon, paprika, cumin and turmeric

500 g (1 lb) root vegetables

2 tablespoons plain flour

50 g (2 oz) sultanas

75 g (3 oz) green or puy lentils

200 g (7 oz) frozen broad beans

1 tablespoon tomato purée

1 litre (1¾ pints) low-salt vegetable stock

pepper

fresh herbs, to garnish (optional)

Couscous
450 ml (¾ pint) boiling water

a few saffron threads

200 g (7 oz) couscous

1 Trim the fat off the lamb and cut the meat into cubes. Heat the oil in a frying pan, add the lamb and onion and fry, stirring, for 5 minutes or until the meat is browned and the onions are golden.

2 Stir in the garlic, cloves and other spices and cook for 1 minute. Dice and mix in the root vegetables, then stir in the flour. Add the sultanas, lentils, broad beans and tomato purée, stir in the stock and a little pepper and bring to the boil.

3 Transfer the mixture to a casserole dish, cover and cook in a preheated oven, 180°C (350°F), Gas Mark 4, for 1½ hours or until the meat is tender.

4 When the tagine is almost ready put the saffron in a bowl, pour over the boiling water and mix together well. Add the couscous, cover and leave to stand for 5 minutes. Fluff up with a fork and spoon on to serving plates. Top with the tagine and garnish with torn herbs, if liked.

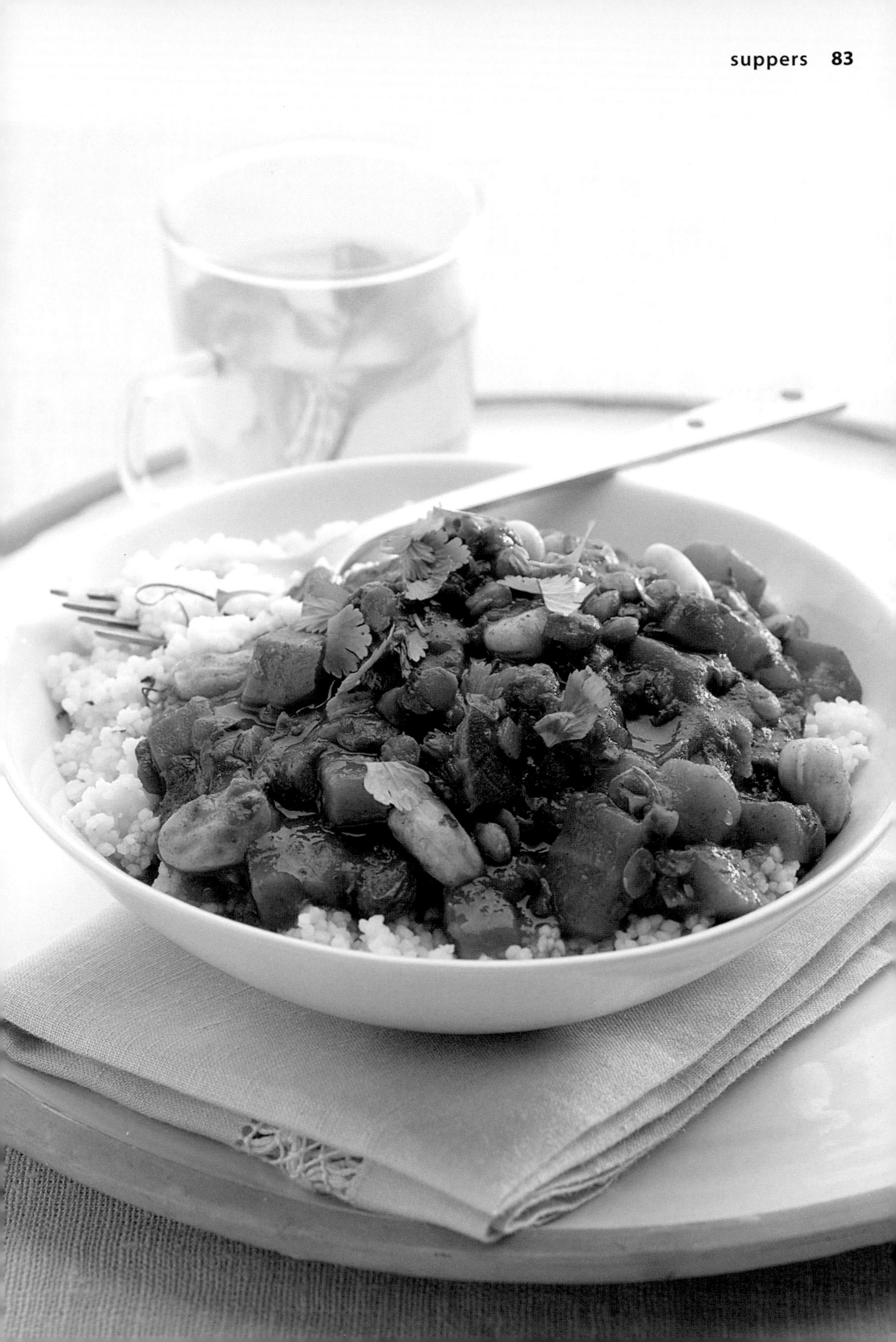

Nutritional values
Kcals 372
fat 9.6 g
saturates 0.9 g
sugars 3.2 g
salt 0.4 g

Preparation time
25 minutes
Cooking time
24–26 minutes
Serves
4

NUTRITIONAL TIP
Steaming is a healthy way of cooking because none of the vitamins or minerals are lost in the cooking water and no additional fat is required to stop the food from sticking as you cook it.

Steamed trout with pesto

Delicately flavoured, pastel pink trout fillets are rolled around a pesto filling, then served on a coarse mash speckled with vibrant green peas and pesto mixed with quark for a creamy taste but without the saturated fat.

625 g (1¼ lb) potatoes, cut into chunks

4 trout fillets, about 625 g (1½ lb) in total, skinned

5 teaspoons basil pesto

175 g (6 oz) frozen peas

100 g (3½ oz) quark soft cheese

pepper

basil leaves, to garnish (optional)

1 Half-fill the base of a steamer with water and bring to the boil. Add the potatoes, cover and cook for 15 minutes.

2 Meanwhile, rinse the fish with cold water and drain well. Put it, skinned side up, on a chopping board and spread each fillet with ½ teaspoon pesto and a little pepper. Roll up loosely, starting from the tail end.

3 Fold up the edges of a piece of foil to make a dish large enough to hold the trout rolls and small enough to sit inside the steamer, leaving space for steam to circulate. Arrange the trout on the foil in a single layer.

4 Put the foil tray in the steamer, on top of the potatoes, add a lid and steam for 6–8 minutes or until the fish flakes easily when pressed with a knife. Add the peas to the potato pan beneath the steamer for the last 3 minutes.

5 Remove the top of the steamer, drain the potatoes and peas, then add the remaining pesto, the quark and a little pepper. Mash coarsely with a fork, then spoon on to 4 serving plates. Arrange the trout on top and sprinkle with basil leaves, if liked.

Nutritional values
Kcals 571
fat 33.5 g
saturates 7 g
sugars 6.2 g
salt 0.6 g
fibre

Preparation time
25 minutes
Cooking time
15 minutes
Serves
4

NUTRITIONAL TIP
Although mackerel is high in fat, it is in the form of omega-3, an essential fatty acid thought to help protect against heart and circulation problems.

Baked mackerel with a herb crust

If you are one of the many people who don't eat mackerel because of the bones, this recipe is for you. These fillets are topped with a tangy lemon and chive ciabatta crust and served with baby new potatoes tossed in a wholegrain mustard dressing.

500 g (1 lb) baby new potatoes, halved

2 large whole mackerel, each cut into 2 fillets

25 g (1 oz) ciabatta or farmhouse white bread

grated rind and juice of ½ lemon

2 tablespoons chopped chives

2 teaspoons olive oil

150 g (5 oz) low-fat natural yogurt

2 teaspoons wholegrain mustard

1 teaspoon clear honey

75 g (3 oz) mixed gourmet salad leaves

pepper

1 Put the potatoes in a saucepan of boiling water and cook for 15 minutes or until tender.

2 Line a large baking sheet with nonstick baking paper. Rinse the fish fillets with cold water, drain them well and put them, skin side down, on the paper.

3 Tear the bread into small pieces or briefly blend in a food processor or liquidizer to make coarse crumbs. Mix with the lemon rind and juice, chives and a little pepper. Spoon over the top of the fish fillets, then drizzle with the oil.

4 Bake in a preheated oven, 220°C (425°F), Gas Mark 7, for 10 minutes or until the fish flakes easily when pressed with a knife and the crumb mixture is golden and crisp.

5 Meanwhile, mix the yogurt, mustard, honey and a little pepper together in a salad bowl. Drain the potatoes and add them to the dressing. Toss together, then add the salad leaves, mix gently and spoon on to serving plates. Add the mackerel and serve immediately.

Nutritional values

Kcals 417

fat 17.2 g

saturates 3 g

sugars 15.4 g

salt 0.4 g

fibre

Preparation time

20 minutes

Cooking time

25 minutes

Serves

4

NUTRITIONAL TIP

Eating salmon is one of the easiest ways to boost your intake of omega-3 fats. If you don't like fresh salmon, use canned salmon instead – it's great as a filling for sandwiches or baked potatoes.

Cajun salmon with beetroot mash

Vibrant, almost electric pink beetroot mash is flavoured with a little root ginger, then topped with grilled salmon steaks rubbed with a Cajun spice blend for a quick family meal or easy supper to share with friends.

500 g (1 lb) raw trimmed beetroot, peeled and cut into chunks

300 g (10 oz) potatoes, peeled and cut into chunks

4 salmon steaks, each about 150 g (5 oz)

1$\frac{1}{2}$ teaspoons ground Cajun spice

4 cm (1$\frac{1}{2}$ inch) piece of fresh root ginger, peeled and finely chopped

2 teaspoons set or clear honey

50 g (2 oz) quark soft cheese

3–4 tablespoons skimmed milk

pepper

steamed green beans, to serve

1 Add the beetroot and potatoes to a saucepan of boiling water and simmer for 20 minutes or until tender.

2 Meanwhile, rinse the salmon steaks with cold water, drain well and put into a foil-lined grill rack. Rub all over with the spice and one-third of the ginger, turn skin side up and drizzle with the honey.

3 Cook the salmon under a preheated hot grill for 10 minutes, turning once or twice and spooning the cooking juices over until the skin is crisp and blackened and the fish flakes when pressed with a knife.

4 Drain the beetroot and potatoes and return to the pan. Mash with the remaining ginger, quark, milk and a little pepper. Transfer to serving plates, top with the salmon, spoon the cooking juices over and serve with steamed green beans.

Nutritional values

Kcals 463

fat 20.7 g

saturates 3.6 g

sugars 13.3 g

salt 1.5 g

fibre

Preparation time

20 minutes

Cooking time

10–13 minutes

Serves

4

NUTRITIONAL TIP

Natural low-fat yogurt is a much healthier alternative to mayonnaise and can be flavoured with chopped red chilli, curry paste, lemon or lime rind.

Warm salmon & bean salad

Even if you aren't really keen on lettuce, prepare to be won over by this chunky, satisfying salad, flecked with large pieces of warm salmon and finished with a garlicky basil dressing to spoon over at the end.

3 salmon steaks, each about 150 g (5 oz)

grated rind and juice of 1 lemon

2 tablespoons olive oil

3 teaspoons set honey

410 g (13½ oz) can haricot or cannellini beans, rinsed and drained

410 g (13½ oz) can of pinto or borlotti beans, rinsed, drained

425 g (14 oz) can artichoke hearts, drained and quartered

50 g (2 oz) pitted olives

2 courgettes, about 300 g (10 oz) in total, diced

125 g (4 oz) sugar snap peas, halved

small bunch of basil

150 g (5 oz) low-fat natural yogurt

1 garlic clove, finely chopped

pepper

1 Rinse the salmon with cold water, then put the steaks in a single layer in the top of an electric steamer or a steamer set over a saucepan of simmering water. Sprinkle with a little of the lemon rind and a little pepper, cover and cook for 8–10 minutes or until the salmon flakes easily when pressed with a knife.

2 Meanwhile, put the remaining lemon rind, lemon juice, oil, 2 teaspoons honey and a little pepper into a salad bowl and fork together. Add the beans to the dressing with the artichoke hearts and olives and toss together.

3 Transfer the salmon to a plate. Add the courgettes and sugar snap peas and steam for 2–3 minutes or until just cooked. Remove the skin from the salmon, then break the flesh into large flakes, removing any bones. Add the green vegetables and salmon flakes to the bean salad along with half the basil, torn into pieces.

4 Toss the salad together, then spoon it on to 4 serving plates. Mix the yogurt with the remaining honey, torn basil leaves, garlic and a little pepper. Spoon into a small bowl and serve with the salmon salad.

Nutritional values

Kcals 395

fat 9.1 g

saturates 4.5 g

sugars 14.5 g

salt 1.3 g

Preparation time

20 minutes

Cooking time

16–17 minutes

Serves

4

✚ **NUTRITIONAL TIP**

Using reduced-fat cheese can significantly reduce the fat content of a dish. Choose a mature cheese rather than a mild variety – that way you won't need to use as much but will still get a strong, cheese flavour

Macaroni cheese

Forget about stodgy school dinners. This colourful version is packed with just-cooked broccoli, leeks and peas bathed in a low-fat cheese sauce flavoured with Dijon mustard and topped with sliced tomatoes and a bubbling cheesy crust.

175 g (6 oz) wholewheat pasta tubes

175 g (6 oz) broccoli, cut into florets

175 g (6 oz) leek, thickly sliced

100 g (3½ oz) frozen peas

40 g (1½ oz) cornflour

750 ml (1¼ pints) skimmed milk

3 teaspoons Dijon mustard

125 g (4 oz) reduced-fat mature Cheddar cheese

2 tomatoes, sliced

15 g (½ oz) fresh Parmesan cheese, finely grated

little paprika

pepper

1 Bring a saucepan of water to the boil, add the pasta and cook for 7 minutes. Add the broccoli and cook for 3 minutes, then add the leeks and peas and cook for 2 minutes or until all the vegetables and pasta are just tender.

2 Meanwhile, mix the cornflour with a little milk in a small bowl to make a smooth paste. Tip into a second saucepan and mix in the remaining milk. Bring to the boil, whisking until thickened and smooth. Stir in the mustard and pepper then three-quarters of the Cheddar.

3 Drain the cooked vegetables and pasta and stir into the sauce. Spoon into a shallow ovenproof dish, cover with the tomato slices, then sprinkle with the remaining Cheddar, the Parmesan and a little paprika.

4 Cook under a preheated grill for 4–5 minutes until the cheese is bubbling and golden. Serve with salad.

Nutritional values

Kcals 402

fat 13.5 g

saturates 2.5 g

sugars 7.7 g

salt 0.6 g

Preparation time

30 minutes

Cooking time

16–20 minutes

Serves

4

NUTRITIONAL TIP

Filo pastry is much lower in fat than other types of pastry. For example, 100 g (3½ oz) frozen shortcrust pastry contains 28.5 g fat and 11.4 g saturates, whereas the same weight of frozen filo pastry contains just 2.7 g fat and 0.3 g saturates.

Filo fish pies

Petal-like open pies are generously filled with a mix of lightly poached fish and bathed in a creamy sauce enriched with fat-free quark instead of cream. Serve with new potatoes and mixed steamed vegetables.

300 g (10 oz) salmon fillet

400 g (13 oz) haddock or cod loin

450 ml (¾ pint) skimmed milk

1 bay leaf

4 teaspoons cornflour

100 g (3½ oz) quark soft cheese

4 spring onions, thinly sliced

100 g (3½ oz) sweetcorn, thawed if frozen

15 g (½ oz) low-fat spread

2 teaspoons sunflower oil

2 sheets of filo pastry, thawed if frozen

pepper

1 Put the fish, milk, bay leaf and pepper into a frying pan. Cover and simmer for about 8 minutes or until the fish flakes easily.

2 Transfer the fish to a plate (leaving the milk in the pan). Bone, skin and flake the flesh into large pieces.

3 Mix the cornflour with a little water to make a smooth paste, then stir it into the milk. Heat, stirring until thickened. Stir in the quark, spring onions and sweetcorn and set aside.

4 Warm the low-fat spread and oil in a small saucepan. Lightly brush the outside of 4 individual metal pudding tins, each 8.5 cm (3½ inches) across, and put them upturned on a baking sheet.

5 Unfold pastry and brush each sheet with the oil mixture. Cut each sheet into 8 squares, so they are a little larger than the base and sides of the tin. Drape a square over an upturned tin, then add a second piece at a slight angle to the first. Repeat to make 4 layers and make 3 more pastry cases. Bake in a preheated oven, 180°C (350°F), Gas Mark 4, for 8–10 minutes.

6 Return the fish to the sauce and reheat. Lift the cases from the tins and transfer to serving plates. Spoon the filling into the cases and serve with new potatoes and steamed vegetables.

Nutritional values

Kcals 484

fat 6.4 g

saturates 1.7 g

sugars 21.1 g

salt 1.6 g

Preparation time

20 minutes

Cooking time

54 minutes

Serves

4

＋ NUTRITIONAL TIP

Butternut squash is a good source of beta-carotene. This nutrient is used to make vitamin A in the body, but it's also an important antioxidant. Good intakes obtained from food have been linked to a reduced risk of heart disease.

Chillied red bean enchiladas

This vegetarian supper has all the flavour of meat filled enchiladas with a cheesy white sauce topping but without the saturated fat.

1 red or orange pepper

200 g (7 oz) cup mushrooms

1 tablespoon sunflower oil

1 large onion, chopped

2 garlic cloves, finely chopped

1 dried or fresh red chilli

1 teaspoon each of cumin seeds, coriander seeds and smoked paprika

625 g (1¼ lb) butternut squash

410 g (13½ oz) can kidney beans

1 teaspoon caster sugar

400 g (13 oz) can chopped tomatoes

300 ml (½ pint) low-salt vegetable stock

8 soft flour tortillas, 20 cm (8 inch) in diameter

250 g (8 oz) quark cheese

40 g (1½ oz) reduced-fat mature Cheddar cheese

pepper

1 Halve, core, deseed and dice the pepper. Trim and slice the mushrooms. Heat the oil in a saucepan, add the onion and fry gently for 5 minutes or until just beginning to brown. Stir in the garlic, peppers and mushrooms and fry for 3 minutes.

2 Halve and deseed the chilli. Crush the cumin and coriander seeds. Deseed and peel the butternut squash and cut into large dice. Rinse and drain the kidney beans.

3 Stir in the chilli, crushed seeds, paprika, butternut squash, kidney beans and sugar, cook for 1 minute, then mix in the tomatoes, stock and a little pepper. Bring to the boil, stirring, then cover and simmer for 15 minutes or until all the vegetables are tender. Discard the chilli.

4 Separate the tortillas and scoop the vegetables on to them using a slotted spoon so that most of the liquid is left behind in the pan. Roll them up, then arrange close together in a roasting tin or shallow ovenproof dish.

5 Drizzle the remaining sauce over the top, especially over the ends of the tortillas. Dot with the quark and sprinkle with the grated Cheddar. Bake in a preheated oven, 190°C (375°), Gas Mark 5, for 25–30 minutes until piping hot and golden on top. Serve with salad.

Nutritional values

Kcals 396

fat 11.2 g

saturates 1.4 g

sugars 9.4 g

salt 1.2 g

Preparation time

15 minutes

Cooking time

25–30 minutes

Serves

4

NUTRITIONAL TIP

Keep your salt levels as low as possible by either making your own stock or using low-salt stock cubes or powdered bouillon.

Quick vegetable balti

Packed with flavour, this mellow-tasting curry can be served simply with warmed naan bread to dunk into the sauce or as part of a larger spread of mixed curries.

200 g (7 oz) long grain brown rice

1 tablespoon sunflower oil

1 onion, cut into wedges

3–4 tablespoons balti or mild curry paste, to taste

1 teaspoon cumin seeds, roughly crushed

1 teaspoon turmeric

2 garlic cloves, finely chopped

4 tomatoes, about 300 g (10 oz) in total, diced

450 ml (¾ pint) low-salt vegetable stock

1 cauliflower, about 500 g (1 lb) when prepared, cut into florets, plus inner green leaves reserved and sliced

410 g (13½ oz) can chickpeas

150 g (5 oz) frozen chopped spinach, thawed

1 Bring a saucepan of water to the boil, add the rice and cook for 25–30 minutes or until tender.

2 Meanwhile, heat the oil in a nonstick frying pan, add the onion and fry for 5 minutes until softened and just beginning to brown. Stir in 3 tablespoons of the curry paste and the cumin, turmeric, garlic and tomatoes. Cook for 1 minute.

3 Mix in the stock, cauliflower and chickpeas, bring to the boil, then cover and simmer for 15 minutes.

4 Add the cauliflower leaves and cook uncovered for 3 minutes. Taste and add extra curry paste, if liked. Add the spinach and cook for 1 minute. Spoon into shallow bowls and serve with the drained rice.

Nutritional values	Preparation time	NUTRITIONAL TIP
Kcals 305	15 minutes	Bacon is high in saturated fat, but
fat 5 g	**Cooking time**	trimming off as much fat as you can
saturates 1.7 g	26–31 minutes	and dry-frying with onion will add
sugars 6.4 g	**Serves**	maximum flavour while keeping fat
salt 1.2 g	4	levels to a minimum.

Tomato, okra & bacon jambalaya

Made with a base of spiced rice, this easy Creole-style fork supper is finished with a mix of okra, green beans and sweetcorn, but do feel free to mix and match your own combinations to use up any leftover vegetables you may have in the refrigerator.

4 rashers unsmoked back bacon, excess fat trimmed away, diced

1 onion, finely chopped

2 garlic cloves, finely chopped

$\frac{1}{4}$ teaspoon cayenne pepper

1 teaspoon paprika

400 g (13 oz) fresh or canned tomatoes, chopped

200 g (7 oz) long grain white rice

750 ml (1$\frac{1}{4}$ pints) low-salt vegetable stock

100 g (3$\frac{1}{2}$ oz) okra, thickly sliced

75 g (3 oz) green beans, each cut into 3 horizontally

75 g (3 oz) frozen sweetcorn

1 Dry-fry the bacon and onion gently in a nonstick frying pan for 5 minutes or until just beginning to turn golden. Mix in the garlic, cayenne pepper, paprika and tomatoes and cook for 1 minute.

2 Stir in the rice and 450 ml ($\frac{3}{4}$ pint) of the stock. Bring to the boil, cover and simmer for 10 minutes, stirring occasionally.

3 Add the okra, beans and sweetcorn, top up with the remaining stock, cover and cook for 10–15 minutes or until vegetables and rice are tender and most of the stock has been absorbed by the rice. Spoon into bowls and serve.

Nutritional values
Kcals 382
fat 8.4 g
saturates 3.2 g
sugars 3.2 g
salt 0.6 g

Preparation time
15 minutes
Cooking time
27 minutes
Serves
4

NUTRITIONAL TIP
Although mature cheese is high in
saturated fat and salt, Parmesan has a
strong flavour, and a little goes a long
way, so you don't need to use as much.

Chillied broccoli & rocket risotto

Wake up your taste buds with this fiery combo of rocket leaves and chopped red
chilli set against a bed of soft, creamy Italian rice and just melting Parmesan.

1 tablespoon olive oil

1 onion, finely chopped

2 garlic cloves, finely chopped

1 red chilli, finely chopped and
deseeded (seeds retained for
extra heat, if liked)

250 g (8 oz) risotto rice

1.5–1.6 litres (2½–2¾ pints) hot
low-salt vegetable stock

150 ml (¼ pint) dry white wine
or extra stock

200 g (7 oz) broccoli, cut into
florets and stem sliced

40 g (1½ oz) rocket leaves

4 tablespoons grated
Parmesan cheese

pepper

1 Heat the oil in a medium-sized saucepan, add the onion
and fry for 5 minutes or until softened and just beginning to
colour. Stir in the garlic and chilli and cook for 1 minute, then
mix in the rice.

2 Add one-quarter of the hot stock, the wine (if used) and a
little pepper, then simmer, uncovered, for 15 minutes, stirring
and topping up with extra stock as needed until the rice is
soft and creamy.

3 Add the broccoli and, if necessary, some extra stock and
cook for 5 minutes or until just tender. Add three-quarters of
the rocket leaves and cook for 1 minute until just wilted, then
spoon into shallow bowls. Sprinkle with the remaining rocket
leaves, a little extra pepper and the Parmesan.

desserts

Nutritional values
Kcals 77
fat 0.1 g
saturates 0.1 g
sugars 13.3 g
salt 0.1 g

Preparation time
30 minutes, plus
freezing and chilling

Serves
6

NUTRITIONAL TIP

Fromage frais is a skimmed-milk soft
cheese that is available in supermarkets,
either as virtually fat free or mixed with
cream. Choose the fat-free version
wherever possible.

Honeyed strawberry mousses

Mini two-tiered mousses with a thin layer of strawberry purée on the top and a
smooth strawberry layer beneath are drizzled with fragrant passion fruit seeds.

3 tablespoons water

**3 teaspoons powdered gelatine
or 1 sachet**

**400 g (13 oz) strawberries,
hulled, plus extra halved
strawberries to decorate
(optional)**

6 teaspoons set honey

**300 g (10 oz) fat-free
fromage frais**

2 passion fruit, halved

1 Put the water in a small cup and sprinkle over the gelatine,
making sure that all the powder absorbs water. Set aside for
5 minutes to soak.

2 Purée half the strawberries with 2 teaspoons honey in a
food processor or liquidizer until smooth, then pour into a jug.

3 Stand the cup of gelatine in a small saucepan of simmering
water and heat until it dissolves and the liquid is clear.

4 Stir 3 teaspoons of the gelatine into the strawberry purée
divide between 6 individual 150 ml (¼ pint) metal pudding
moulds. Chill in the freezer for 15 minutes until just set.

5 Purée the remaining strawberries with the remaining
honey. Add the fromage frais and blend together.
Gradually mix in the remaining gelatine and pour over
the set strawberry layer in the pudding moulds. Chill for
4–5 hours until set.

6 Turn out the desserts by dipping each mould into just-
boiled water, count to 5, loosen the edges with a fingertip,
then invert each mould on to a small plate. Holding plate
and mould, jerk to release the mousse. Repeat with the other
moulds. Spoon passion fruit seeds around the desserts and
decorate with halved strawberries, if liked.

Orange-scented pears & sauce

Quick and easy to make, this dessert is smart enough to serve to friends or simple
enough to make for a midweek supper. It can be made earlier in the day and
warmed through just before serving or at the last minute.

2 oranges

1 cinnamon stick, halved

450 ml (¾ pint) water

25 g (1 oz) caster sugar

**6 firm dessert pears, about
875 g (1¾ lb) in total**

Chocolate sauce
**100 g (3½ oz) plain dark
chocolate, broken into pieces**

6 tablespoons skimmed milk

**large pinch of ground
cinnamon**

1 tablespoon caster sugar

1 Finely grate the rind of one of the oranges and reserve for
the sauce. Pare the rind off the other orange with a vegetable
peeler and cut it into thin strips. Squeeze the juice from both
oranges. Put the juice and strips of rind into a medium-sized
saucepan with the cinnamon stick, water and sugar. Heat
gently until the sugar has dissolved.

2 Peel the pears, then cut down through the stalk to the base,
leaving the stalk on. Scoop out the cores with a teaspoon. Add
the pears to the syrup and simmer gently for 10 minutes or
until tender, turning once or twice with a spoon so that the
halves cook evenly.

3 Lift the pears out of the syrup and put on to a plate. Boil the
syrup for 3 minutes to reduce it slightly, then return the pears
to the pan and leave to cool.

4 Make the sauce. Put 2 teaspoons of the reserved grated
rind into a small saucepan with the chocolate, milk, ground
cinnamon and sugar. Heat gently, stirring occasionally, until
the chocolate has melted and the sauce is smooth and glossy.

5 Arrange 2 warm pear halves in each of 6 shallow serving
bowls, spoon over the orange strips and syrup and drizzle
over the warm chocolate sauce.

Nutritional values
Kcal 299
fat 6.3 g
saturates 2.1 g
sugars 40.4 g
salt 0.4 g

Preparation time
25 minutes
Cooking time
30 minutes
Serves
6

✚ **NUTRITIONAL TIP**
Choosing naturally sweet fruit means you won't need to add as much sugar to puddings. This is good news, as too much sugar can raise levels of a type of blood fat called triglycerides.

Apple strudel pie

If you love pies and pastries, being on a low-cholesterol diet could make you feel that you must avoid these favourites completely. Brushing wafer-thin filo pastry with a little low-fat spread and oil will create a pie that keeps saturated fat to the minimum.

25 g (1 oz) caster sugar

1 teaspoon ground cinnamon

75 g (3 oz) sultanas

6 Gala dessert apples, cored and sliced

20 g (¾ oz) low-fat olive oil spread

1 tablespoon sunflower oil

4 sheets filo pastry, thawed if frozen

sifted icing sugar, to decorate

low-fat custard, to serve

1 Mix together the sugar, cinnamon and sultanas in a large bowl. Add the apple slices and toss them in the sugar mixture.

2 Warm the low-fat spread and oil together in a small saucepan or microwave on full power for 15 seconds. Unfold the pastry and brush a sheet with a little of the spread and oil mixture. Drape it over a 24 cm (9½ inch) enamel pie plate so that the pastry overhangs the plate and on to the work surface. Brush a second sheet of filo and add it at a slight angle to the first. Repeat with another sheet.

3 Pile the fruit mixture in the centre of the pastry-lined plate, cover with the remaining sheet of pastry and fold the edges up and over the top, crumpling the top until the apples are completely covered.

4 Brush the top of the pastry with any remaining oil mixture and bake in a preheated oven, 180°C (350°F), Gas Mark 4, for 40 minutes, covering the top of the pie loosely with foil after 20 minutes so that it doesn't overbrown.

5 Dust the top with a little sifted icing sugar, cut into wedges and serve warm with spoonfuls of low-fat custard.

Nutritional values

Kcals 171

fat 0.2 g

saturates 0 g

sugars 42.2 g

salt 0.1 g

Preparation time

25 minutes

Cooking time

23–30 minutes

Serves

4

NUTRITIONAL TIP

Although this pudding is virtually fat free, remember that any accompaniments, such as custard or ice cream, may not be! Read the labels first.

Spiced apple & meringue

Sometimes we all yearn for a hot, comforting pudding, especially in winter. Although traditional, high-fat, steamed puddings and pastries are now off the menu, you can safely enjoy this zesty hot apple dessert topped with spiced meringue.

8 Gala dessert apples, about 1 kg (2 lb) in total

grated rind and juice of 1 lemon

4 cloves

3 egg whites

25 g (1 oz) caster sugar

25 g (1 oz) light muscovado sugar

¼ teaspoon ground cinnamon

1 Peel, core and thickly slice the apples and put them in a saucepan with the lemon rind and juice and cloves. Add 6 tablespoons water, cover and simmer gently for 8–10 minutes until the apples are just tender.

2 Put the egg whites into a large mixing bowl and whisk until stiffly peaking. Mix together the caster and muscovado sugars and cinnamon and gradually whisk into the egg whites a teaspoon at a time. Continue to whisk the meringue for a couple of minutes until it is thick and glossy.

3 Transfer the apples to a 1.2 litre (2 pint) pie dish. Spoon over the meringue and swirl the top with the back of the spoon. Bake in a preheated oven, 160°C (325°F), Gas Mark 3, for 15–20 minutes until the topping is set and crusty on the outside and soft in the centre. Spoon into bowls.

Nutritional values

Kcals 106

fat 0.3 g

saturates 0.1 g

sugars 22.1 g

salt 0.1 g

Preparation time

20 minutes, plus chilling

Cooking time

2–3 minutes

Serves

6

NUTRITIONAL TIP

This dish is completely fat free, low in calories and packed with vitamin C, thanks to all the fruit it contains.

Orange, grapefruit & mango jellies

Refreshingly tangy, this light dessert is made by mixing blood red orange juice with pieces of mango and grapefruit and orange segments and topping with spoonfuls of sweetened fromage frais.

2 oranges

1 ruby grapefruit

1 large ripe mango

2 tablespoons water

2 teaspoons powdered gelatine

450 ml (¾ pint) blood- red orange juice

200 g (7 oz) fat-free fromage frais

1 tablespoon icing sugar

1 Cut the top and bottom off each orange and the grapefruit with a small serrated knife and use the knife to cut the peel away from the sides of the fruit. Holding the fruit over a bowl, cut between the membranes to release the segments. Squeeze the juice from the membrane into the bowl.

2 Stand the mango on its side and cut a thick slice off each side to reveal the stone in the central slice. Cut the flesh away from the stone, peel the fruit and cut the flesh into slices.

3 Put the water in a small bowl and sprinkle the gelatine over the top, making sure that all the powder absorbs water. Leave to stand for 5 minutes, then heat the bowl in a saucepan half-filled with water until the gelatine has dissolved and the liquid is clear and straw coloured.

4 Gradually stir the gelatine into the orange juice. Spoon the fruit into 6 glass tumblers, adding any juice to the gelatine mixture, then pour this evenly into the tumblers, leaving some of the fruit sticking out of the top. Chill for 4 hours or longer, if needed, until set.

5 Mix the fromage frais with the icing sugar in a small bowl and allow diners to spoon some on top of the jellies as they are about to eat.

Nutritional values
Kcals 191
fat 1.1 g
saturates 0.3 g
sugars 27.3 g
salt 0.2 g

Preparation time
10 minutes
Cooking time
1¾ hours
Serves
4

✚ NUTRITIONAL TIP
Using short grain brown rice will increase fibre levels, helping to fill you up so you're not tempted to munch on fatty and sugary snacks later in the day.

Rice pudding with roast apricots

Make full use of the oven when you are cooking a casserole and cook this quick-to-prepare, store cupboard pudding on the shelf below.

65 g (2½ oz) pudding or short grain rice

2 tablespoons caster sugar

grated rind of 1 lemon

600 ml (1 pint) skimmed milk

little grated nutmeg

Roast apricots
6 fresh apricots, halved and stoned

juice of 1 lemon

4 cardamom pods

1 tablespoon caster sugar

1 Put the rice and sugar into a 1.2 litre (2 pint) pie dish, add the sugar and lemon rind and pour over the milk. Sprinkle the top with a little grated nutmeg.

2 Bake in a preheated oven, 160°C (325°F), Gas Mark 3, for 1¾ hours or until the top is golden and the rice is tender. If the rice is very runny, leave the pudding to stand at room temperature for 10 minutes before serving.

3 About 20 minutes before the end of cooking put the apricots, cut side up, into a shallow ovenproof dish and drizzle over the lemon juice. Crush the cardamom pods and add the black seeds and pods to the stone cavities. Sprinkle with sugar and roast on the oven shelf above the pudding for 10–15 minutes until heated through and just beginning to soften.

4 Spoon the rice pudding into bowls and add the apricots to the side.

Nutritional values

Kcals 274

fat 8.4 g

saturates 1.7 g

sugars 33.3 g

salt 0.2 g

Preparation time

25 minutes

Cooking time

30–35 minutes

Serves

6

NUTRITIONAL TIP

Puddings are a great way to get one of your five a day portions of fruit and vegetables. The plums in this dish still count, even though they are cooked.

Ruby plum clafoutis

Traditionally made with cherries, this popular French dessert is rather like a sweet and fruity version of Yorkshire pudding. Only a tiny amount of oil is used to grease the baking tin, so this makes a great alternative to high-fat tarts and sponge puddings.

oil for greasing

500 g (1 lb) red plums, quartered and stoned

75 g (3 oz) caster sugar

grated rind and juice of ½ small orange

75 g (3 oz) plain flour

3 eggs

1 teaspoon vanilla extract

450 ml (¾ pint) semi-skimmed milk

sifted icing sugar, to decorate

6 scoops reduced-fat vanilla ice cream, to serve

1 Lightly oil a 23 cm (9 inch) square cake tin or 20 x 25 cm (8 x 10 inch) roasting tin. Add the plums, sprinkle with 1 tablespoon sugar and the orange juice and set aside.

2 Meanwhile, put the remaining sugar and flour into a mixing bowl, add the eggs, vanilla extract and orange rind and whisk until smooth. Gradually whisk in the milk until the batter is smooth and frothy. Set aside for 30 minutes.

3 Bake the plums in a preheated oven, 190°C (375°F), Gas Mark 5, for 10 minutes. Whisk the batter again briefly, then pour it into the tin of hot plums. Quickly return the pudding to the oven and bake for 30–35 minutes until well risen and golden-brown. Dust with sifted icing sugar and serve immediately with vanilla ice cream.

Nutritional values

Kcals 78

fat 0.2 g

saturates 0 g

sugars 19.7 g

salt 0 g

Preparation time

30 minutes,

plus freezing

Cooking time

10 minutes

Serves

6

NUTRITIONAL TIP

Granita is completely fat free and is a great heart-healthy alternative to ice cream.

Blackberry & apple granita

Refreshingly tangy flakes of fruity ice make a deliciously light summer dessert and look pretty served in dainty glasses topped with a few extra blackberries. For a special touch, try drizzling with a little vodka or crème de cassis just before serving.

600 ml (1 pint) water

25 g (1 oz) caster sugar

4 large Gala apples, about 650 g (1 lb 5 oz) in total, unpeeled, cored and diced

150 g (5 oz) blackberries

1 Pour half the water into a saucepan, add the sugar and bring slowly to the boil, stirring until the sugar has dissolved.

2 Add the fruit, cover and simmer for 10 minutes until the apples are tender. Leave to cool for 15 minutes.

3 Purée the fruit mixture until smooth, mix with the remaining water and tip into a nonstick roasting tin so that the mixture is about 2.5 cm (1 inch) deep. Freeze for 1½–2 hours until mushy.

4 Beat the mixture with a fork to break up the large ice crystals and return to the freezer for 2 hours, beating at 30 minute intervals until fine icy flakes have formed. Spoon into glasses to serve.

Nutritional values

Kcals 169

fat 0.2 g

saturates 0.1 g

sugars 39.6 g

salt 0.2 g

Preparation time

30 minutes

Cooking time

52–53 minutes

Serves

6

NUTRITIONAL TIP

Fat-free, strained Greek yogurt is now readily available in most supermarkets. If you can't find it, use fat-free fromage frais or low-fat set natural yogurt instead.

Ginger meringues with ruby grapes

Individual pavlovas speckled with peppery-tasting crystallized ginger are topped with a syrupy compote of ruby grapes cooked in red grape juice. They may look like a classic pavlova, but fat-free yogurt has been spooned under the grapes, not double cream.

2 egg whites

100 g (3½ oz) caster sugar, plus 1 tablespoon

½ teaspoon cornflour

½ teaspoon white wine vinegar

½ teaspoon vanilla extract

25 g (1 oz) crystallized ginger, finely chopped

300 g (10 oz) ruby seedless grapes, halved

175 ml (6 fl oz) red grape juice

300 g (10 oz) fat-free Greek yogurt

1 Line a large baking sheet with nonstick baking paper. Whisk the egg whites in a large, dry bowl until stiffly peaking. Gradually mix in the 100 g (3½ oz) of sugar, a teaspoonful at a time, and once all the sugar has been added continue whisking for 1–2 minutes until thick and glossy.

2 Mix together the cornflour, vinegar and vanilla extract in a small bowl, then fold into the meringue. Fold in the ginger.

3 Spoon the meringue into 6 mounds on the baking sheet, spreading them into swirly circles about 8 cm (3½ inches) across. Make a slight dip in the centre of each. Bake in a preheated oven, 120°C (250°F), Gas Mark ½, for 45 minutes or until the meringues can be easily peeled off the paper. Leave to cool on the paper.

4 Meanwhile, put the grapes, grape juice and 1 tablespoon sugar into a small saucepan and simmer for 5 minutes or until just tender. Lift out of the pan with a slotted spoon, then boil the syrup for 2–3 minutes until reduced to 3 tablespoons. Return the grapes to the pan and leave to cool.

5 Transfer the meringues to 6 serving plates. Spoon the yogurt on top and arrange the grapes and syrup on top of that. Serve within 30 minutes of assembly.

Nutritional values

Kcals 177

fat 0.8 g

saturates 0.1 g

sugars 16.6 g

salt 0.3 g

Preparation time

15 minutes

Cooking time

Serves

6

NUTRITIONAL TIP

This dessert is low in fat and is a good alternative to traditional bread and butter pudding, which is made with eggs, butter and milk.

Mini summer puddings with vodka

Forget about lining a pudding basin and leaving it to soak for hours on end. This speedy alcoholic version of a favourite summer dessert can be assembled in minutes for a dainty finale to any supper party.

12 slices wholemeal bread

500 g (1 lb) frozen mixed summer berries, just thawed

50 g (2 oz) caster sugar

6 tablespoons vodka

200 g (7 oz) fat-free fromage frais

1 Use a fluted biscuit cutter to cut a 7 cm (3 inch) circle from each slice of bread. Discard the remaining bread.

2 Drain the juices from the thawed fruit into a shallow bowl, then dip each side of the bread circles into the juice. Place a circle of bread on each of 6 small serving plates.

3 Mix the fruit with the sugar and vodka, then spoon two-thirds of the mixture on to the bread circles on the plates. Cover with the remaining dipped bread slices. Serve within 30 minutes of making, spooning the remaining fruits over at the last minute and accompanying with spoonfuls of fromage frais.

Nutritional values
Kcals 154
fat 6.1 g
saturates 0.9 g
sugars 17.3 g
salt 0.1 g

Preparation time
45 minutes
Cooking time
15 minutes
Serves
6

Fruit salad cups

If you serve this pretty dessert to friends, they will never guess that you are on a special diet. Dainty French-style tuile biscuits, filled with a mixture of mango, raspberries and blueberries, and spoonfuls of low-fat Greek yogurt.

2 egg whites

50 g (2 oz) caster sugar

3 tablespoons sunflower oil

few drops vanilla extract

40 g (1½ oz) plain flour

1 large mango

150 g (5 oz) fresh raspberries

100 g (3½ oz) blueberries

200 g (7 oz) fat-free Greek yogurt

sifted icing sugar, to decorate

1 Line 3 baking sheets with nonstick baking paper. Put the egg whites in a bowl and fork together until frothy but still clear. Add the sugar, oil and vanilla extract and mix together.

2 Sift the flour into the bowl and stir together. Spoon the mixture into 6 mounds on the baking sheets and spread each to a circle, about 12 cm (5 inches) across.

3 Bake one of the baking sheets in a preheated oven, 190°C (375°F), Gas Mark 5, for about 5 minutes until the biscuits are light brown in the centre and slightly darker around the edges. Remove from the oven and leave to stand for 30 seconds. Put a second tray in the oven.

4 Loosen the cooked biscuits. Working quickly, drape each biscuit over a large orange and pinch the edges to make a fluted edge. Leave to set for a few minutes then lift off the oranges, turn up the other way and put on to a wire rack. Repeat to make 6 cups.

5 Stand the mango on its side and cut a thick slice off each side. Cut the flesh away from the stone and peel and cut the flesh into slices. Mix with the berries. Spoon the yogurt, then the fruit into cups. Transfer to serving plates and dust with icing sugar. Serve immediately.

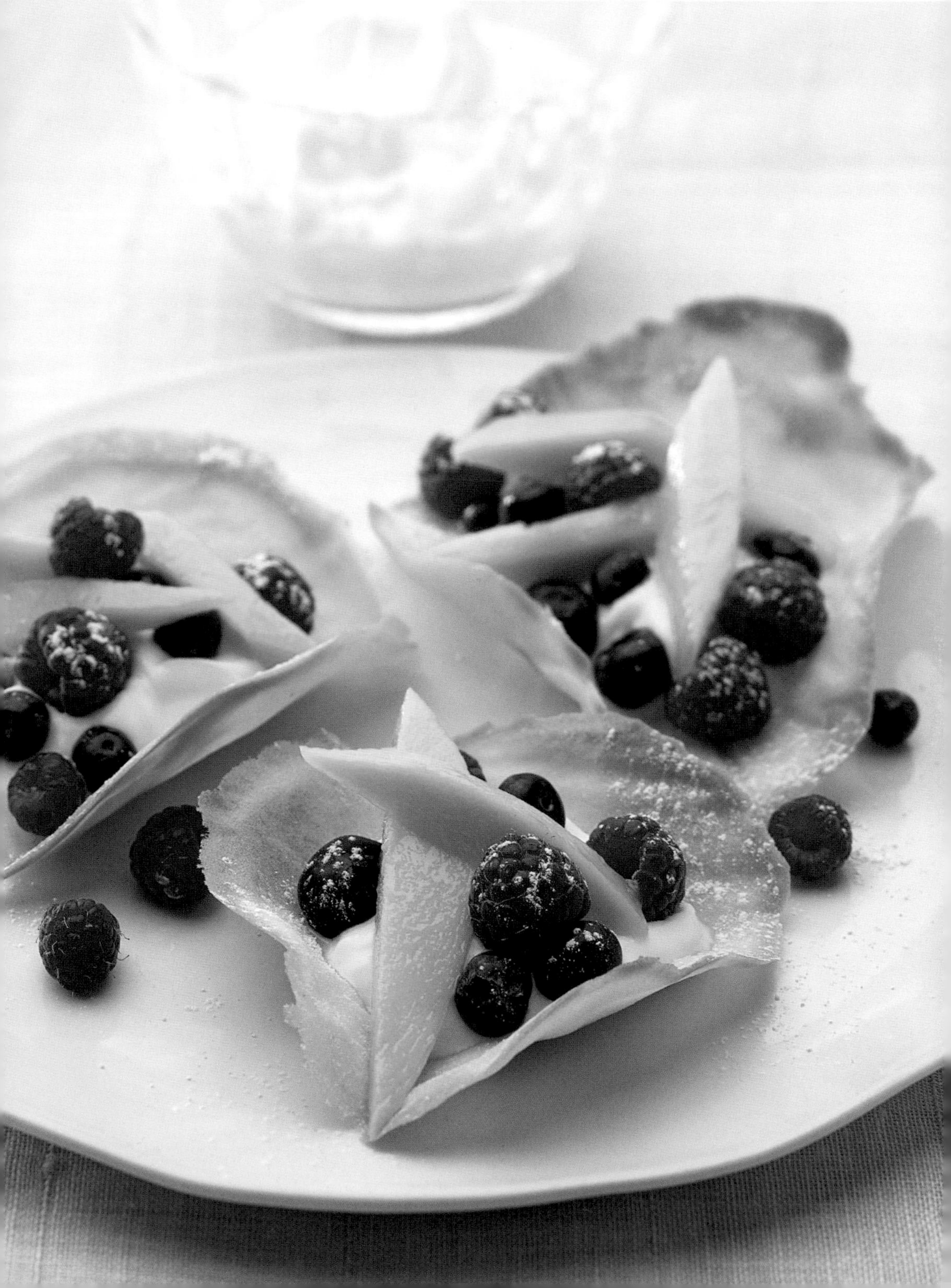

cakes and bakes

Nutritional values
Kcals 201
fat 3.1 g
saturates 0.9 g
sugars 23.9 g
salt 0.1 g

Preparation time
30 minutes
Cooking time
20 minutes
Serves
8

NUTRITIONAL TIP
Egg yolks do contain some saturated fat, but compared with a sandwich cake made with butter and eggs this is still a much healthier option.

Summer berry roulade

Old-fashioned baking at its best: just a few ingredients, well cooked and simply served. Perfect with a cup of tea.

4 eggs

125 g (4 oz) caster sugar, plus extra for sprinkling

grated rind of 1 lemon

125 g (4 oz) plain flour

Filling
250 g (8 oz) fat-free fromage frais

125 g (4 oz) quark

1 tablespoon caster sugar

125 g (4 oz) blueberries

150 g (5 oz) raspberries

1 Line the base and sides of a 30 x 23 cm (12 x 9 inch) roasting tin with a single sheet of nonstick baking paper, cutting the paper in the corners. Put the eggs, sugar and lemon rind in a mixing bowl set over a saucepan of simmering water. With an electric whisk, beat the mixture for 10 minutes until it is thick and the mixture leaves a trail over the surface when the beaters are raised.

2 Remove the bowl from the saucepan, sift the flour over the surface and gently fold. Pour the mixture into the tin. Bake in a preheated oven, 200°C (400°F), Gas Mark 6, for 8–10 minutes until the top springs back when pressed with a fingertip.

3 Wet a clean tea towel with hot water, wring it out then put it on the work surface with a narrow edge towards you. Cover it with a piece of nonstick baking paper and sprinkle with sugar. Quickly turn the sponge out on to the paper, peel off the lining paper and cover with a second piece of paper. Loosely roll up the sponge, starting from the edge nearest you. Leave loosely wrapped in the sugared paper to cool.

4 Unroll the sponge and remove the centre paper. Mix the fromage frais and quark with the sugar and spread over the cake. Sprinkle with the fruit, reserving a few for decoration, reroll the sponge and transfer to a serving plate. Decorate with the remaining fruit and serve cut into thick slices.

Nutritional values
Kcals 117
fat 0.6 g
saturates 0.1 g
sugars 14.5 g
salt 0.2 g

Preparation time
10 minutes
Cooking time
12–15 minutes
Makes
15 cakes

NUTRITIONAL TIP
These rock cakes use fat-free fromage frais rather than butter, which slashes the fat content but not the taste.

Pineapple & ginger rock cakes

A childhood favourite with a Caribbean twist, these quick and easy cakes are best eaten while still warm from the oven. Instead of butter, they are made with fromage frais, a skimmed milk soft cheese similar in texture to yogurt.

sunflower oil, for oiling

250 g (8 oz) self-raising flour

75 g (3 oz) caster sugar

75 g (3 oz) fat-free fromage frais

1 egg

227 g (7½ oz) can pineapple rings in natural juice, drained and chopped

75 g (3 oz) glacé cherries, roughly chopped

4 teaspoons chopped glacé ginger

2 tablespoons demerara sugar or extra caster sugar, to decorate

1 Lightly brush 2 large baking sheets with a little sunflower oil. Put the flour, sugar, fromage frais and egg into a bowl, add the pineapple, cherries and ginger and fork together until just mixed.

2 Spoon 15 roughly shaped mounds on to the baking sheets, sprinkle with demerara or extra caster sugar and bake in a preheated oven, 190°C (375°F), Gas Mark 5, for 12–15 minutes until golden. Leave to cool slightly, then transfer to a serving plate. These rock cakes are best eaten on the day that they are made.

Nutritional values

Kcals 176

fat 11 g

saturates 1.4 g

sugars 7.8 g

salt 0.1 g

Preparation time

10 minutes

Cooking time

20 minutes

Makes

10 bars

NUTRITIONAL TIP

Oats are a great source of cholesterol-lowering soluble fibre. In fact, studies show that eating oats can help to lower blood cholesterol levels a little.

Nutty flapjack bars

Quick and easy to make, these healthy flapjacks are perfect to add to an office lunchbox and unlike their bought counterparts they are additive free and much lower in sugar.

4 tablespoons olive oil

50 g (2 oz) light muscovado sugar

175 g (6 oz) banana, weighed with skin on

50 g (2 oz) mixed nuts, such as whole almonds, pecans and hazelnuts

2 tablespoons sunflower seeds

2 tablespoons pumpkin seeds

100 g (3½ oz) rolled oats

1 Line the base and sides of a shallow 18 cm (7 inch) square baking tin with a single piece of nonstick baking paper, cutting into the corners. The paper should be a little above the edges of the tin. Put the oil and sugar in a saucepan and heat gently until the sugar has melted.

2 Peel and mash the banana and stir into the oil mixture with the remaining ingredients.

3 Tip the mixture into the tin and press into an even layer. Bake in a preheated oven, 180°C (350°F), Gas Mark 4, for about 20 minutes until golden-brown. Leave to cool and harden in the tin.

4 Lift the flapjacks from the tin by holding the paper. Transfer to a chopping board and cut into bars, peeling off the paper as you go. Store in an airtight tin for up to 3 days.

Nutritional values

Kcals 58

fat 2.8 g

saturates 0.2 g

sugars 7.2 g

salt 0 g

Preparation time

15 minutes

Cooking time

15 minutes

Makes

26 macaroons

+ NUTRITIONAL TIP

Macaroons make a sweet alternative to biscuits, but are a better choice for a healthy heart because they don't use butter or egg yolks, both of which contain fat and saturates.

Hazelnut macaroons

These dainty biscuits are delicious served with steaming mugs of strong black coffee or frothy cappuccino, or you could enjoy them them as an accompaniment to Blackberry and Apple Granita (see page 110).

100 g (3½ oz) hazelnuts

25 g (1 oz) icing sugar

150 g (5 oz) caster sugar

4 teaspoons ground rice

2 egg whites

13 whole hazelnuts to decorate

1 Line 2 large baking sheets with rice paper, shiny side up. Grind the nuts in a liquidizer or food processor or chop them very finely with a knife.

2 Put the ground nuts, icing and caster sugars and ground rice in a bowl and mix with the egg whites.

3 Pipe or spoon heaped teaspoons of the mixture on the baking sheets, spacing them well apart. Add half a hazelnut to the centre of each.

4 Bake in a preheated oven, 160°C (325°C), Gas Mark 3, for about 15 minutes until pale golden. Leave them to cool, then break away the extra paper surrounding the biscuits and discard it. Serve now, while crisp, or store overnight in a cake tin for a softer, chewier centre.

Nutritional values

Kcals 212

fat 1.5 g

saturates 0.4 g

sugars 29.9 g

salt 0.4 g

fibre

Preparation time

20 minutes,

plus soaking

Cooking time

50–60 minutes

Makes

10 slices

+ NUTRITIONAL TIP

Using mashed bananas helps to keep this cake moist, sweet and tasty, without the need to add butter or too much sugar.

Light banana fruit cake

Fruit cakes are traditionally made with butter, but this version has no added fat at all and just very small amounts in the eggs. It is made by soaking dried fruit in hot tea and then mixing in mashed bananas for extra moistness and sweetness.

250 g (8 oz) **luxury dried fruit**

250 ml (8 fl oz) **hot black tea**

grated rind of 1 orange

175 g (6 oz) **bananas, weighed with the skin on**

100 g (3½ oz) **light muscovado sugar**

250 g (8 oz) **self-raising flour**

1 teaspoon **baking powder**

1 teaspoon **ground cinnamon**

2 **eggs, beaten**

1 Put the fruit into a large bowl with the hot tea and orange rind and leave to soak for 4 hours. Line the base and sides of a 20 cm (8 inch) springform tin with nonstick baking paper or greaseproof paper. If using greaseproof paper, lightly brush the paper with oil.

2 Peel and mash the bananas and add to the soaked fruits with the sugar, flour, baking powder and cinnamon. Add the eggs and mix together.

3 Spoon the mixture into the lined tin, spread the top level and bake in a preheated oven, 160°C (325°F), Gas Mark 3, for 50–60 minutes or until golden-brown, the top has risen and cracked and a skewer inserted into the centre of the cake comes out cleanly.

4 Leave to cool for 10 minutes, remove the tin, transfer the cake to a wire rack and peel away the lining paper. Leave to cool completely, then cut into slices to serve. Store in an airtight tin and eat within 3 days.

index

acknowledgements

For more information about familial hypercholesterolemia (FH) contact HEART UK (see page 4 for contact details)

To find your BMI visit the British Dietetic Association's Weight Wise website www.bdaweightwise.com

For more information on drinking sensibly visit www.drinkaware.co.uk

Executive Editor Nicola Hill
Editor Lisa John
Deputy Creative Director Karen Sawyer
Designer Beverly Price, www.one2six.com
Photographer William Lingwood
Food stylist Sara Lewis
Props stylist Liz Hippisley
Picture Library Manager Jennifer Veall
Production Controller Nigel Reed
For Heart UK Michael Livingston, Linda Main, Gill Stokes

picture credits